The Dialectical Method Of Biblical Exegesis

A Revelation Paradigm for Students Taught By the Holy Spirit - Studying Scripture

Abe Johnson, Jr.

Volume 1

CTP

Central Truth Publisher, Tallahassee, Florida, and Trafford Publishing, Canada

A note from Central Truth Publishers:
We believe and affirm God's vision to provide the local church with trained ministers and Christian workers using biblical models to evangelize, make disciples and to minister in the home, the church, the community and the world. It is our prayer that this publication will help readers discover a dependence on the Holy Spirit for Bible study rather than philosophies, language competencies or study methods. For more information, please visit www.scbc.edu.

All Scripture quotations, unless otherwise suggested, are from the
Authorized King James Version.

Edited by Disciple Mittie P. Johnson
Cover image of bible by Derek Lowell Johnson, used with permission.

The Dialectical Method of Biblical Exegesis: A Revelation Paradigm for Students Taught by the Holy Spirit - Studying Scripture © 2003 by Abe Johnson, Jr. All rights reserved. Printed in Canada. You may not copy this book (beyond that allowed by the copyright law) without the original publisher's permission. This applies to reproductions, translations, microfilms, storage, and processing in electronic systems. Contact the author in care of Trafford Publishing.

Trafford Publishing's edition by arrangement with Central Truth Publishers, a ministry of Smith Chapel Bible College, Telecom Center 4085 Bothwell Terrace Tallahassee, Florida 32317

National Library of Canada Cataloguing in Publication

Johnson, Abe, 1951-
   The dialectical method of biblical exegesis : a revelation paradigm for students taught by the Holy Spirit studying scripture / Abe Johnson.
Includes bibliographical references and index.
ISBN 1-4120-0318-0 (v. 1)
   1. Bible--Criticism, interpretation, etc. I. Title
BS511.3.J63 2003   220.6   C2003-902509-8

TRAFFORD

This book was published *on-demand* in cooperation with Trafford Publishing.
On-demand publishing is a unique process and service of making a book available for retail sale to the public taking advantage of on-demand manufacturing and Internet marketing.
On-demand publishing includes promotions, retail sales, manufacturing, order fulfilment, accounting and collecting royalties on behalf of the author.

Suite 6E, 2333 Government St., Victoria, B.C. V8T 4P4, CANADA
Phone   250-383-6864   Toll-free   1-888-232-4444 (Canada & US)
Fax   250-383-6804   E-mail   sales@trafford.com
Web site   www.trafford.com   TRAFFORD PUBLISHING IS A DIVISION OF TRAFFORD HOLDINGS LTD.
Trafford Catalogue #03-0687   www.trafford.com/robots/03-0687.html

10   9   8   7   6   5   4   3

DEDICATION
To my Darling Wife, Disciple Mittie P. Johnson

I would like to give special thanks to my wife for her love, faith, support and Christian virtues. She is my constant source of encouragement and inspiration that has made completing this book possible.

I am forever grateful to Mittie for her many, many hours of work in reviewing the final draft and making recommendations for improvement. She continues to share Scriptural insights that she receives while depending on the Holy Spirit for illumination.

ACKNOWLEDGMENT

I would like to express my gratitude to those students who embraced this new study paradigm, especially Felisa McQueen-Lawson who kept a history of every revision of the dialectical study sheets. I would also like to thank Mother Joyce Rolle for allowing me to set up a memorial scholarship fund in honor of her late husband, Dr. Reginald Rolle. He served as an apologist by allowing his biblical insights to strengthen the new paradigm during our many hours of study. He had a passion for studying without end; and even during his illness, he was a constant source of inspiration. I will always cherish the memory of my dearest friend and colleague, the late Dr. Reginald Rolle.

NOTE:
The editor and I have sought to remove inconsistencies and errors of scriptural references, notes, indexes and charts used throughout this publication. Some will have crept in, for which I take full responsibility. The considerate reader would do me a great service by calling my attention to any such errors or omissions.

Abe Johnson – publisher@scbc.edu

To my Students at Smith Chapel Bible College

SHALOM, Y'SHUA HAMASHIACH ADONAI,
(Peace, our Lord Jesus Christ)

Contents

Title Page

Publication and Copyright Page

Dedication		3
Acknowledgment		4
Introduction		7
1.	The Study Method	17
2.	Textual, Historical, Literary Context	23
3.	Contextual Inquiry	30
4.	Applying Exegetical Methods	35
5.	Exegetical Inquiry	41
6.	List Exegesis	45
7.	Decode Exegesis	55
8.	Narrative Exegesis	65
9.	Epistle Exegesis	77
10.	Miracle Exegesis	86
11.	Prophecy Exegesis	94
12.	Prayer Exegesis	104

13.	Dialog: Using Web Forums	112

Conclusion 116

Bibliography 119

Appendix
    I.   Dialectical Study Sheet   121
    II. Literary Forms Quick Chart   129
    III. The Seven Exegetical Methods   130

Index of Charts 140

Index of Exegesis 141

Index of Figures of Speech 144

Study Resources
    A. Apostle Creed /Scriptural   147
    B. Gospel Jubilee   150
    C. Teaching Principles of Giving   151
    D. Prayers of the Bible   152
    E. Eschatology Study Notes   153
    F. Basic Sermon Outline   166

Introduction

Introduction to the Problem - In *The Open Bible Companion* by Dr. Kenneth Boa, he outlines what he calls prerequisites of Bible study.

He lists the following prerequisites: plan, discipline, dependence, responsiveness, honesty and exposure. His explanation of the prerequisites of dependence not only helped to clarify my own struggles with biblical study, but also helped me to recognize similar struggles of associate ministers. Dr. Boa defines the prerequisite of dependence in this way:

We need a plan for Bible study, and we need the discipline to follow through with that plan so it will become a habitual part of our lives. The plan is only good when followed with a conscious sense of dependence on the teaching and illuminating ministry of the Holy Spirit (John 16:13-15). We must combine discipline (human responsibility) with dependence (divine sovereignty) as we approach the Scriptures. We cannot properly understand or respond to biblical truths in our own power; this requires the grace of God. [1]

I agree with Dr. Boa's understanding of a need for a plan for Bible study. His lineal idea of combining discipline with dependence, however, lacks as a plan for Bible study, in today's postmodern culture. Let me explain this problem. Using Dr. Boa's approach, combining discipline (human responsibility) and dependence (divine sovereignty), let us examine a familiar passage.

Introduction to the Problem

Study to show thyself approved unto God, a workman that needeth not be ashamed, rightly dividing the word of truth, II Timothy 2:15.

Beginning with discipline (human responsibility) it is easy to understand that even without additional Scriptural evidences; Paul penned this topic expecting Timothy, the individual letter recipient, to understand and accept the requirement for disciplined study. In addition, combining dependence (divine sovereignty) the New Testament church as a communal recipient expects not only to understands the same requirement but also define its practical task.

Collectively, the church continues to fail in this endeavor. One way to address this failure is to correct the relationship between discipline and dependence. A new paradigm is one way to carry out this task. For example, the *Dialectical Method of Biblical Exegesis: A Revelation Paradigm for Students Taught by the Holy Spirit - Studying Scripture* (Dialectical Method) offers an alternative. Since, this paradigm changes the lineal relationship between discipline and dependence to that of a hierarchical relationship, it places the Holy Spirit (hierarchically) at the center of all Biblical Studies (John 14:26).

Without being overly simplistic, for the New Testament church to embrace this new paradigm, it must be able to answer at least five questions raised by the text. First, who are the students? Second, what is meant by God's approval? Third, who is the teacher? Fourth, what is the method of study? Fifth, what are the source documents for study?

Introduction to the Problem

Consulting existing educational data is a good starting point. The Integrated Postsecondary Education Data System (IPEDS) runs under the National Center for Education Statistics (NCES). IPEDS uses a system of surveys designed to collect data from all primary providers of postsecondary education including hundreds of Bible colleges, seminaries and religious universities. If religious education serves the purpose of the local church, then one would expect a relationship other than monetary support or sponsorship. Besides, if religious colleges and universities are handling discipline (human responsibility) then the local churches' agenda should be one of dependence (divine sovereignty).

A review of collected data shows a seemingly disconnect between the (divine sovereignty) of the local churches and the religious colleges and universities they support or sponsor. This is self-evident when conducting a peer analysis of mission statements, programs of study or degrees offered by religious colleges and universities.

Developing a new paradigm to address the questions raised by the text would bridge the gap between the local churches and the mission of the training institution they support. This book is an attempt to solve that disconnect. This research is a direct response to II Timothy 2:15 and the questions it raise by addressing the hierarchical relationship that exists between discipline and dependence.

Review of the Research

Review of the Research - A general void exists in the research about the prerequisite for Bible study. One exception is Dr. Kenneth Boa's acknowledgment of the need for these prerequisites. Research available on related topics includes the process of Bible study, various study methods and types of exegesis. The research reviewed, though helpful, does not address the pragmatic task of training institutions governed by, or ministries of, the local church working in a paradigm shift.

This paradigm shift by definition is where the religious colleges and universities view the post-secondary institution as the bastion of divine authority rather than the local church. Given the specific task of this research and the broad base of primary literature on study methods, I am also painfully aware of how incomplete this study remains. The authors cited in the bibliography and notes represent a fraction of the literature, which I have reviewed.

Implication of the Research - First, a trend worthy of consideration is the insatiable need for the Word of God. This may be both a blessing and a curse. The blessing supports a basic need of civilization for spiritual growth and the curse supports spreading modern English revisions of the Bible. Second, I agree with Dr. Boa's assessment that, "Many believers associate Bible study with drudgery; limiting themselves to mere samples, they never cultivate a true taste for it contents. There are two basic reasons for this problem: lack of a proper *motivation* and lack of a proper *method*." [2]

Implications of the Research

Moreover, my ministry to churches located in Atlanta, Georgia, Memphis, Tennessee, and Tallahassee, Florida, served as the theological womb for developing a proper method. To some extent, this new theoretical paradigm limits study mainly for use with the *Authorized King James Version* and translations based on the received text. Nonetheless, it offers more than just another method of study, but a method that depends solely on the Holy Spirit's ministry for illumination.

Testing the Dialectical Method at Smith Chapel Bible College's seven Schools of Excellence provided a qualitative testing ground for developing both its educational and pedagogical models. Professors using the Dialectical Method underscored dependence on the Holy Spirit for illumination rather than philosophy, language competencies, or academic discipline, taught more than three-hundred and fifty students from various churches. This included students attending both Church based Training Centers and SCBC Cyber Campus on the Worldwide Web.

There are roughly one hundred graduates since 1991 who currently use the Dialectical Method in ministry. Sunday school teachers, who are graduates of SCBC, at the Revival Center Church of Outreach Ministries, Havana, Florida, for example, have adopted the Dialectical Method as the only teaching tool for the adult classes. Furthermore, both current students and alumni continue to report satisfaction of personal growth as they move from Bible knowledge to Biblical revelation.

Theoretical Framework

The Dialectical Method also encourages a sharpening of God-given abilities to develop Bible based models for Christian church ministries, as shown by several churches and related ministries started by members of SCBC National Alumni Association. In addition, the Dialectical Method continues to promote rapid spiritual growth that continues to equip believers for ministry in the home, the church, the community and the world.

Sharing the Dialectical Method with the community of faith about the truth of the Holy Spirit's ministry in Biblical study is my highest priority. My choice of the *Authorized King James Version* of the Bible brings a sharp focus to the outcome of this research. I also recognize that with so many present-day revisions of the English Bible and various study methods, the narrow aim of this research may not benefit every student of Scripture. I am confident, however, that those students, who might benefit from this research, will eventually affirm a dependence on the ministry of the Holy Spirit for Scriptural illumination.

Theoretical Framework - The Dialectical Method has six sections. *Section one* is the study method. This section defines the Dialectical Method, sets forth its goal and objectives and gives Scriptural foundation for its existence. At this point, the Bible student is ready for section two.

Section two discovers the textual, historical and literary context. This section begins with a text. The text when placed within its context allows discovery of the literary form. On discovery, the context referred to as the study passage is self-evident.

Theoretical Framework

Further, examination of the study passage's background, panoramic view and rules for study outside the context also helps illuminate the study passage. The Bible student is ready to move on to section three.

Section three is the contextual inquiry and has three items of inquiry. Item one confirms the main speaker, teacher, preacher, or writer. This inquiry helps to discover whether the passage content is the words or deeds of God, Satan, demons, angels or man. Item two confirms the authority issues about any claims, divine call, or commission of the Biblical character. A prophet, for example might carry more authority than that of a king or perhaps even a priest, depending on the context. Item three confirms the audience taking part in the historical events, along with any response. Completing this inquiry makes section four easy.

Section four applies one of the seven exegetical methods, namely: list, decode, narrative, epistle, miracle, prophetic and prayer exegesis designed to discover the Central Truth. With this discovery, the Bible Student is ready for section five.

Section five is the exegetical inquiry and has three items of inquiry. Item one confirms whether the central truth of the study passage is literally or figuratively. Item two confirms its prophetic view, which focuses on one of the following: the Church, the World or Israel. Item three confirms its profitability, namely, doctrine, reproof, correction, or instruction in righteousness. The Bible student is now ready for section six.

Purpose of the Study

Section six is extending the dialog using web forums. This section is only accessible on the Worldwide Web by login in a password-protected directory. These supervised forums designed to encourage a study of the Bible invite apologists from the community of faith to take part in and add to the effectiveness of the Dialectical Method. The basis of the online discussions is as follows:

Knowing this first, which no prophecy of the scripture is of any private interpretation. For the prophecy came not in old time by the will of man: but the holy men of God spake as they were moved by the Holy Ghost (2 Peter 1:20, 21).

The Purpose of the Study - This research does not address current issues related to any debate about the reliability or inerrancy of the *Authorized King James Version*. This research addresses neither politically correct nor culturally acceptable issues about the use of gender bias references. These issues, though valid, are beyond the scope and intent of this research. In addition, my claims of independent research and revelation should be self-evident as implied, rather than the reader expecting a critical review of " Hegel B.W.F: *The Philosophical System*." [3]

Does the title of the book Dialectical Method present an oxymoron to the study of the Holy Bible? Dr. Earle E. Lee, President of the Florida Council of Private Colleges, Inc., asked this probing question during a pre-publication discussion. Dr. Lee stated, "Hegel's thesis, antithesis and synthesis model is a contradiction, in that, revelation truth is absolute and has no opposite or antithesis, therefore a synthesis is not possible."

Research Questions and Design

Finally, no one can publish or make such statements as I have made without being aware of the probing question asked by Dr. Lee, along with other philosophical dangers attending the enterprise. This includes the possibilities for misreading, misuse, serving one's own self-interest, and the fallacy of dependence on God for what seems obvious in Scripture. I engage readers, therefore, to the same challenge to which I challenge students in the classroom: **depend solely on the Holy Spirit to illuminate Scripture.** My desire is not that this research circumvents other excellent study methods, but that it promotes students' dependence on God's Spirit for biblical revelation rather than the collective wisdom of civilization. I invite those who may not view the ministry of the Holy Spirit as essential for Biblical study as I do, to embrace the testimony of Apostle John:

For I testify unto every man that heareth the words of the prophecy of this book, If any man shall add unto these things, God shall add unto him the plagues that are written in this book:
And if any man shall take away from the words of the book of this prophecy God shall take away his part out of the book of life, and out of the holy city, and from the things which are written in this book (Revelation 22:18,19).

Research Questions and Design - The research questions are as follows: First, who are the students? Second, what is the meaning of approval to God? Third, who is the teacher? Fourth, what is the method of study? Finally, is the Bible the only source documents for study? The research design follows the general approach, specifically the case study method. The Dialectical Method provides answers for my research questions.

Research Questions and Design

Notes

1. Boa Kenneth D, *The Open Bible Companion*, Thomas Nelson Publishers, 1986: p.72. This spiral-bound publication is the complete (out of print) guide to getting the most from your Open Bible for lesson, study, and sermons.
2. *Ibid.*, p. 71.
3 Hegel G.W.F.: *The Philosophical System*. Contributors: Howard P. Kainz - author. Publisher: Ohio University Press, 1998: p. iii. HEGEL, Georg Wilhelm Friedrich (1770-1831). One of the most influential of the 19th-century German philosophers, Georg Wilhelm Friedrich Hegel also wrote on psychology, law, history, art, and religion. Karl Marx based his philosophy of history on Hegel's law of thought, called the dialectic. In this dialectic an idea, or - *thesis*, contains within itself an opposing idea, called - *antithesis*. Out of the inevitable conflict between these opposing concepts is born a third, new thought, the synthesis. Applied to history by the Marxists, Hegel's concepts advanced the notion of the class struggle. From the strife over the ownership of the means of production would arise a new classless society the - *synthesis*.

The significance of Hegel's ideas stems in part from the fact that they apply not only to abstract thoughts but also to psychology, religion, and history. An essential element of his system was his belief that the grasp of reality happens when examined as a whole and that any attempt to discover truth by scrutinizing a single facet of reality is doomed to failure.

As the author, I appreciate the historical contributions by Hegel; however, the reference merely gives him credit for the term dialectical method as the title of this publication rather than the content of this research. I am also grateful for Hegel's idea of "reality happens when examined as a whole" as I have used this idea to construct the *Dialectical Method of Biblical Exegesis: A Revelation Paradigm for Students Taught by the Holy Spirit Studying Scripture*.

A Blessed and Sacred Journey

The

Celebration

of

Life

for

Sister Joyce Cassandra Mills-Robinson

"To everything there is a season and a purpose for every matter under heaven"

~ *A Time to be Born and a Time to Die* ~
September 23, 1948 – April 5, 2009

Saturday, April 11, 2009
2:30 O'clock P.M.

Rock Hill MB Church
Proctor Road
Tallahassee, Florida

Sister Joyce's Final Resting Place and Her New Home

2nd Corinthians 5:1
"For we know that if our earthly house of this Tabernacle is dissolved, we have a building of God. A house not made with hands, eternal in the heavens."

Flower Attendants
Rock Hill Ushers and Friends

Honorary Pallbearers
Deacon Arthur Mills   Deacon Albert Mills
Deacon Tommy Mills   Brother Joseph Mills
Brother Tarek Julius

Active Pallbearers
Brother Tracy V. Holton
Brother Alfred Simmons
Brother Shawn Holton
Deacons of Rock Hill MB Church

Interment
Rock Hill Cemetery
Tallahassee, Florida

Our Gratitude
We, the family, sincerely convey our deepest gratitude to all of you who found so many tender ways to express your concern, love and sympathy. Because of your kindness, we thank God for friends like you. The Mills-Robinson Family

Repass
Rock Hill MB Church Fellowship Hall

Culley's MeadowWood Funeral Home
Tallahassee, Florida

Obituary

Joyce Cassandra Mills-Robinson, 60, passed away Sunday, April 5, 2009 in Annandale, VA.

Joyce was born September 23, 1948 in Leon County to the late Shelly Mills, Sr. and Mary Speed Mills. She was educated in Leon County schools.

Joyce was converted and received the gift of the Holy Ghost. She answered her call to the Ministry in the office of an Evangelist, Praise and Worship Leader for many years thru out the counties. She was a member of Family Worship Center, Springfield, VA since 1998.

She leaves to cherish her memory, three children, Timothy F. Reynolds, Sr. of Bingham, NY, and Dewayne Williams (Jonita) and Dawn F. Gallon (Michael), both of Tallahassee; six grandchildren, Timothy Lewis Jemmison, Tiere C. Brack, Sabryia A. Reynolds, Aniscia S. Clark, Timothy Reynolds, Jr., and Michael A. Gallon, Jr., two brothers, Arthur Mills (Louise) of Apalachicola and Albert Mills (Exxie) of Port Arthur, TX; two sisters, Lizzie Mills-Wright of Tampa and Lillie Ruth Mills of Apalachicola; one brother-in-law, Jay Sewell of Moss Point, MS; several uncles, two aunts, and a host of nieces, nephews, cousins and friends including her niece, Elder Carrie Holton.

She was preceded in death by her parents, and six siblings, Solomon Mills, Sr., Annie Lee Holton, Tommie Mills, Shelly Mills, Jr., Elmira Sewell, and Leroy Mills.

~~~~~

"Why Was I Here?"
Written by Carrie Holton
(Based on a writing by Maureen Edwards)

I was here because of love; I was a woman full of freedom from above. I was intuitive, I was an over comer in life's challenges. I was not alone, for I had many spiritual family members who kept me covered in their prayers. I was confident in the woman I was. I had nothing to prove to anyone. I was not defined by size, the shade of my hair nor was I defined by clothes, car, or my past. I was defined by God's image, in which He created me. So, I would have said, I was a survivor, I was a motivator, I was a friend, I was a daughter, I was a mother, I was a sister, I was an aunt, I was a cousin, I was a niece. BUT, most of all, I was a daughter of a King (Jesus).

I leave with you today, my future generation: Timothy, DeWayne, Dawn and my beloved grandchildren; and all who shall remember me, to remember the good times we may have shared and remember the blessings that were always there. Most of all, remember that struggles are just for the moment and joy comes in the morning. So I say, "Good Morning"!
I will see you one day in another fellowship morning around the Throne of God!

Order of Divine Worship and Remembrance

Joyce has taken a journey on the beautiful ship of rest, far away from this world of sorrow, to her home of eternal rest. And now we pray, "Dear God give us strength to bear it, and courage to fight the blow; because what it means to lose her, no one will ever know."

~~~~~

Presiding	Pastor Michael Willia...
Processional	Family and Frier...
A Hymn of Praise	Deacon Tommy ...
A Prayer of Remembrance	Deacon in Ch...
Song of Praise	Rock Hill ...
Scriptures of Praise New Testament	Pastor Arthur Ste...
Old Testament	Pastor Michael W...
Solo	
Reflections and Tributes	Anyone (limit two minutes,...
Acknowledgements and Resolutions	Sister K...
A Song of Praise	Rock H...
Words of Comfort	Elder Leroy ...
And they went out......	

📖 Chapter 1

Study Method

Section one is the study method. This section defines the Dialectical Method, sets forth its single goal, two objectives and gives Scriptural foundation for its existence.

What is the Dialectical Method? The Dialectical Method is a Revelation Paradigm for Students Taught by The Holy Spirit - Studying Scripture. Understanding a revelation paradigm is pivotal in defining the Dialectical Method. During my many years of ministry, I have discovered four levels of revelation that help to understand the purpose of a revelation paradigm.

Level one is information. Both saints and sinners receive information through the ear and the eye gate. Since the fall of man (Genesis Chapter 3), ninety-five percent of all information is worthless. This conclusion, reached because of all the wisdom or actions of civilization since the fall, highlight the sin nature of man. Five percent of the time God's mercy and grace interacts with fallen man. The realization of God's mercy and grace is hidden until after the new birth and a life style of Biblical Christianity becomes self-evident. Let us take an example where information is available about NASA's historic moon landing and the planting of an American Flag. Though historic, not all embrace this information, and skeptics are on record as doubting NASA's and television networks' claims.

Study Method

Level two is knowledge. Knowledge requires self-verification. Earning a college degree, for example, or getting a computer technician certificate, holding a plumber's license all require gaining knowledge. Knowledge, therefore, is that which is gained by hearing or observation. Using the example of NASA's landing on the moon, what is the question?

Who has knowledge of this event? The astronauts whose feet touched the moon have knowledge of this event. Therefore, what is knowledge to the astronauts is merely information to the masses.

Level three is Bible knowledge. If Bible knowledge is the opposite of knowledge, what is Bible knowledge? Bible knowledge requires faith in that which we have not heard or viewed. For example, the Bible declares the power of God raised Jesus from the dead (Acts 2:24). Believers alive today were not there to hear about it or view it, yet accept it as truth. This is faith. Romans 10:9-10 teaches that Bible knowledge is God's first contact for the redemption of civilization. The passage reads thus:

That if thou shalt confess with thy mouth the Lord Jesus, and shalt believe in thine heart that God hath raised him from the dead, thou shalt be saved. For with the heart man believeth unto righteousness; and with the mouth confession is made unto salvation (Romans 10:9-10).

Level four is revelation truths. The believers spiritual progress from Bible knowledge and faith to revelation truths and works requires the New Birth experience (2 Corinthians 5:17).

Study Method

Bible knowledge about the New Birth becomes revelation truth about the new birth: "If I am in Christ, [I am a New Creature...."]. The brackets indicate the personal revelation of the Biblical Text. This New Birth opens the door for an individual to discover revelation paradigms.

Level five is revelation paradigm. The first interaction of God in the affairs of civilization reveals His perfect will and plan for all, in every age. The revelation paradigm when discovered, allows the believer to judge truth from error.

For example, let us examine the revelation paradigm for marriage (Genesis 2:24). *First,* God's artistry shows His skill, handiwork, capacity, creativity, inventiveness, composition, refinement and excellence in painting civilization a portrait of marriage. This we called His first masterpiece (Adam and Eve). *Second,* civilization needs to make a copy of the portrait of marriage painted by the God of Creation. *Third,* man must leave his father and mother and find gainful employment and satisfactory finances. *Fourth,* man must CLEAVE (**C**are, **L**ove, **E**agerly **A**dmire and **V**ivaciously **E**njoy his wife). Finally, man must be one flesh. This fulfills the command to "... *be fruitful and multiply.*" (Genesis 1:28). In addition, the Dialectical Method itself a revelation paradigm, reveals the Holy Spirit as our teacher (John 14:26).

Study Method

What is the goal and objectives of the Dialectical Method? The goal requires affirmative answers to two questions: First, do you seek revelation rather than just Bible knowledge? Second, do you receive that: *"wisdom is the principle thing; therefore get wisdom: and with all thy getting get understanding"* (Proverbs 4:7"). There are two tasks in understanding the goal; namely, *seeking revelation* and the preparation for *receiving wisdom*.

In the first task *seeking revelation* as a *Tabula Rasa* is a pre-condition for receiving it. This approach allows the Holy Spirit to write revelation truths on the heart. The emphasis on the ministry of the Holy Spirit, rather than worldly wisdom, requires a New Birth (John 3:6-7). The events recorded in (Acts 2:1-41) reveal the revelation paradigm for the Holy Spirit ministry in carrying out the New Birth.

First, the Word goes forth (Acts 2:14-36.). The theme is "Jesus Lives", in (Acts 2:24) Peter used his sermon to convince the hearer about the truth of Jesus of Nazareth incarnation and His bodily resurrection.

Second, Faith (Acts 2:37a) indicates the "prick" which signals a "cut" or deposit. This activation of Faith is the genuine response to the Word (Romans 10:17). Faith is a Ministry of the Holy Spirit.

Third, repentance (Acts 2:38a) is the evidence of faith. Where there is no turning to God and away from sin, there is no faith. Therefore, we go back to step one - preaching the Word. Sinners continue to sin. Repented sinners live righteous and holy.

Study Method

Fourth, Holy Spirit Baptism (Acts 2:38b, c) as pointed out in this verse teaches an event secured in Heaven before revealed on Earth. The Holy Spirit lives only in clean vessels. For example, "Baptism in the Name of Jesus," the word "in" in this passage as well as many others denotes relationship. Therefore, repentance and remission of sin only take place in a relationship with Jesus. This spiritual baptism is an immersion into the Body of Christ and a confirmation of repentance. *Fifth*, Water Baptism (Acts 2:41.) is a public witness or testimony to our Spirit Baptism. Without a Spirit Baptism, our Water Baptism is in vain.

In summary, beginning with the preached Word of God, the Holy Spirit takes the revelation truth of the Word and inserts it into the spirit of man. Faith is man's response to the Word. The evidence of faith is repentance. The Holy Spirit baptism confirms repentance, giving a clean vessel in which the Spirit of God lives. Finally, water baptism is a public witness of Holy Spirit baptism.

In the second task, preparing to *receive wisdom* is the principle thing. Preparation requires prayerful study, expecting revelation truths necessary for understanding the present-day application of each passage. Reaching this goal requires performing two tasks: seeking revelation and receiving wisdom. This is the result of meeting the two objectives of the Dialectical Method.

There are two objectives required to reach the goal of the Dialectical Method. The first objective is to engage Holy Scripture *Authorized King James Version* while prayerfully depending on the Holy Spirit for illumination, rather than wisdom of the world.

Study Method

The second objective is to learn the Biblical relationship between "study and rightly dividing" the Word of truth (2 Timothy 2:15-16). Both objectives underline the quality and quantity of scriptural illumination that depends on time spent prayerfully studying. These objectives help define the Dialectical Method as solely the ministry of the Holy Spirit. What is the Scriptural foundation for its methodology? The building blocks of the Dialectical Method consist of four scriptures that define the terms as used in the title.

1. **Students** - *Ye have not chosen me, but I have chosen you, and ordained you, that ye should go and bring forth fruit, and that your fruit should remain: that whatsoever ye shall ask of the Father in my name, he may give it you.* (John 15:16), **taught by the**

2. **Holy Spirit** - *But the Comforter, which is the Holy Ghost, whom the Father will send in my name, he shall teach you all things, and bring all things to your remembrance, whatsoever I have said unto you* (John 14:26).

3. **Studying** - *Study to shew thyself approved unto God, a workman that needeth not to be ashamed, rightly dividing the word of truth. But shun profane and vain babblings: for they will increase unto more ungodliness* (2 Timothy 2:15, 16).

4. **Scripture** - *All scripture is given by inspiration of God, and is profitable for doctrine, for reproof, for correction, for instruction in righteousness: That the man of God may be perfect, thoroughly furnished unto all good works* (2 Timothy 3:16, 17).

Chapter 2

Determining the Textual, Historical, Literary Context

Section two discovers the textual, historical and literary context. This section begins with a text. The text placed within its context based on form of composition, background, and panoramic view. This section also addresses contextual rules for study outside the context.

The text, when using the Dialectical Method, is the Scripture verses read – the beginning of Scripture, the starting point for the study. The text is a single verse, John 3:16; Psalm 150; or a chapter, for example, containing the Lord's Prayer, John 17. When Scripture is read, quoted, cited, sung or written it becomes the text. The text is always out of context until discovery of the context based on its literary forms. Let us examine a passage of scripture (Matthew 13:31-32) and review the study sections of the Dialectical Method.

The Text -

Another parable put he forth unto them, saying, The <u>kingdom of heaven</u> is like to a grain of mustard seed, which a man took, and sowed in his field:

Which indeed is the least of all seeds: but when it is grown, it is the greatest among herbs, and becometh a tree, so that the birds of the air come and lodge in the branches thereof (Matthew 13:31b-32). Note: The parable begins with the phrase "The Kingdom of heaven …" rather than, at the beginning with "Another parable put he forth unto then, saying …."

Textual, Historical, Literary Context

The text, also known as the study passage is out of context. The next requirement is to put the text back into its proper context. The context is synonymous with literary form and often referred to as the form of composition. Understanding literary forms helps us to read, interpret, and make application of biblical truths. A working knowledge of biblical literature helps in rightly dividing the word of truth (2 Timothy 2:15-16). A good publication is Long Thomas G, *Preaching and the Literary Forms of the Bible*, Fortress Press, 1990.

The Context -
Another parable put he forth unto them, saying, The <u>kingdom of heaven</u> is like to a grain of mustard seed, which a man took, and sowed in his field:
Which indeed is the least of all seeds: but when it is grown, it is the greatest among herbs, and becometh a tree, so that the birds of the air come and lodge in the branches thereo (Matthew 13:31b-32.)

The Literary Form -
The literary form, for the passage is a *parable* (short story with hidden moral or spiritual meaning). It begins in verse 31b, and ends in verse 32. In this study, the context is the same as the text. In many other instances, but not all, the passage may suggest another literary form. Please see Appendix II, p., 129 for a quick technical chart for discovering literary forms. Based on literary form, the Bible has three biblical classifications. The first biblical classification is the covenant principles. This covenant, in general, is between God and Israel. These principles begin in Genesis and end in Malachi. The Decalogue (Genesis Chapter 20) serves as a historical road map of God's contact with His people.

📖 Chapter 2

Determining the Textual, Historical, Literary Context

Section two discovers the textual, historical and literary context. This section begins with a text. The text placed within its context based on form of composition, background, and panoramic view. This section also addresses contextual rules for study outside the context.

The text, when using the Dialectical Method, is the Scripture verses read – the beginning of Scripture, the starting point for the study. The text is a single verse, John 3:16; Psalm 150; or a chapter, for example, containing the Lord's Prayer, John 17. When Scripture is read, quoted, cited, sung or written it becomes the text. The text is always out of context until discovery of the context based on its literary forms. Let us examine a passage of scripture (Matthew 13:31-32) and review the study sections of the Dialectical Method.

The Text -

Another parable put he forth unto them, saying, The <u>kingdom of heaven</u> is like to a grain of mustard seed, which a man took, and sowed in his field:

Which indeed is the least of all seeds: but when it is grown, it is the greatest among herbs, and becometh a tree, so that the birds of the air come and lodge in the branches thereof (Matthew 13:31b-32). Note: The parable begins with the phrase "The Kingdom of heaven ..." rather than, at the beginning with "Another parable put he forth unto then, saying ...."

Textual, Historical, Literary Context

The text, also known as the study passage is out of context. The next requirement is to put the text back into its proper context. The context is synonymous with literary form and often referred to as the form of composition. Understanding literary forms helps us to read, interpret, and make application of biblical truths. A working knowledge of biblical literature helps in rightly dividing the word of truth (2 Timothy 2:15-16). A good publication is Long Thomas G, *Preaching and the Literary Forms of the Bible*, Fortress Press, 1990.

The Context -
Another parable put he forth unto them, saying, The <u>kingdom of heaven</u> is like to a grain of mustard seed, which a man took, and sowed in his field:
Which indeed is the least of all seeds: but when it is grown, it is the greatest among herbs, and becometh a tree, so that the birds of the air come and lodge in the branches thereo (Matthew 13:31b-32.)

The Literary Form -
The literary form, for the passage is a *parable* (short story with hidden moral or spiritual meaning). It begins in verse 31b, and ends in verse 32. In this study, the context is the same as the text. In many other instances, but not all, the passage may suggest another literary form. Please see Appendix II, p., 129 for a quick technical chart for discovering literary forms. Based on literary form, the Bible has three biblical classifications. The first biblical classification is the covenant principles. This covenant, in general, is between God and Israel. These principles begin in Genesis and end in Malachi. The Decalogue (Genesis Chapter 20) serves as a historical road map of God's contact with His people.

Textual, Historical, Literary Context

The second biblical classification is the kingdom principles. These principles begin in Matthew and end in John. Often quotations used by Jesus from the covenant principles introduced into the kingdom, using one or more of his teaching formulas, become kingdom principles. The beatitudes (Matthew 5:1-12) set forth the preamble to the kingdom principles. The gospel accounts, in general, reveal a continuity of the struggle between the spirit of religion (civilization centered) and the spirit of revelation (God centered) as it started in (Genesis Chapter 3).

The third biblical classification is the Christian principles. These principles begin in Acts and end in Revelations. The principles taken from both the covenant and kingdom make application in the New Testament church mostly through the epistle writers. Understanding these three biblical classifications leads us to the next requirement of the Dialectical Method, valid considerations using contextual rules for going outside the context.

Contextual Rules -
Contextual rules set forth the limits for the study of each passage. Remember when placing the passage in context, based on literary forms, it is necessary to preserve both a contextual relationship and the continuity of revelation between passages from a different context. This is true even when the study passage comes from a passage of a separate set of biblical principles. With this in mind, there are four valid reasons for going outside the context of the study passage.

Textual, Historical, Literary Context

- First, consider the passage composition that uses citations, quotes, or application of revelation truth from prior passages.

- Second, consider the passage composition that uses prophetic literature. An examination of fulfilled prophecy requires the inclusion of references to its fulfillment while unfulfilled prophecy requires a "Time Line of Bible Prophecy" (Please refer to Appendix III, Chart 10-1 summary of End Time Events p. 138 and Eschatology Notes p. 153).
- Third, consider the passage composition when answering questions in Section three - contextual inquiry.
- Fourth, consider whether the passage has parallel or synoptic events recorded in Scripture.

A careful examination of Matthew 13:31b, 32 reveals the application of two rules requiring going outside the context. They are Rule no. 2 and 4. Let us examine each rule for clarification.

Rule no 2 - A Scriptural reference for Isaiah 2:2, 3 listed in the *Authorized King James Version* for Matthew 13:31, is showed by the (<u>*underlined phrase*</u>) in the study passage. A close examination of the Isaiah reference reveals the passage composition used in Matthew 13:31. It also provides a prophetic link to the prophecy of Isaiah. This prophetic link frames a valid reason for going outside the context under Rule No 2. Let us examine the two passages linked prophetically as shown by the underlined words.

Textual, Historical, Literary Context

Chart 1-1

KINGDOM/COVENANT PRINCIPLES	
Classification: Kingdom Principles	Classification: Covenant Principles
Another parable put he forth unto them, saying, The <u>kingdom of heaven</u> is like to a grain of mustard seed, which a man took, and sowed in his field: Which indeed is the least of all seeds: but when it is grown, it is the greatest among herbs, and becometh a tree, so that the birds of the air come and lodge in the branches thereof (Matthew 13:31-32).	*And it shall come to pass in the last days, that the mountain of the <u>LORD'S house</u> shall be established in the top of the mountains, and shall be exalted above the hills; and all nations shall flow unto it. And many people shall go and say, Come ye, and let us go up to the mountain of the LORD, to the house of the God of Jacob; and he will teach us of his ways, and we will walk in his paths: for out of Zion shall go forth the law, and the word of the LORD from Jerusalem* (Isaiah 2:2, 3).

Rule no 4 - A parallel account, mainly used while studying the events of the four gospels considers the perspectives of more than one writer recording the same event or teaching. Having the same central truth or moral point confirms parallel accounts. Some events or teachings are similar but not parallel. This is when different moral points about teachings or outcomes of events are obviously different. A careful examination of the context may reveal the writer using a literary device that records an (expanded version) of a parable or event, in one context, for example, and only the moral point or outcome (condensed version) in another.

Textual, Historical, Literary Context

This is also referred to as a parallel event or teaching. Please refer to Holdcroft Thomas L, *The Four Gospels*, Third Edition, CeeTeeC Publishing, 1999 for discussion of the four gospels. In the study passage, both Mark and Luke record parallel account.

Chart 2-2

PARALLEL OR SYNOPTIC ACCOUNTS		
MATTHEW	MARK	LUKE
13:31, 32	4:30, 32	13: 18, 19

Background -

The background gives us the stage or setting in which the event took place. Look for such events as the changing from one location to another, or giving a revelation to more than one group. The best reference requires checking the outline in the *Authorized King James Version*, Study Bible edition. Also, see Mears, Henrietta C. *What the Bible is All About, Regal Books,* 1997 for outline information. Discover the background by examining the outline for Matthew 13:31-32 using more than one reference. Let examine the passage outline chart on the next page.

Textual, Historical, Literary Context

Chart 3-3

RESULTS OF JESUS REJECTION	
- Parable of the Soils	13:1-23
- Parable of the Wheat and Tares	13:24-30
- Parable of the Mustard Seed	13:31, 32
- Parable of the Leaven	13:33-35

This outline continues with three more parables spoken to the disciples: The parable of the tares explained, hidden treasure and pearl of great price. In addition, there are two miracle narratives of both sight and speech, Matthew 13:36-53. The background for the parable of the mustard seed is part of Matthew's collection of parables spoken to the multitude. Therefore, the narrow background is Matthew 13:1-35. On the other hand, the broad background collects parables to both the multitude and the disciples. This background is Matthew 13:1-53. It is a good idea to consider both the narrow and the broad background, when studying, teaching or preaching from the four gospels.

Panoramic View -

The panoramic view confirms the author, collection of literature, theological themes, custom and traditions of the Holy lands, first response of the hearers and relevant topography. The minimum consideration is the author and collection of literature. Matthew listed as an apostle, is the author of the Book (Matthew 10:1-4). Please refer to Laney Carl J, *Concise Bible Atlas: a Geographical Survey of Bible History*, Hendrickson Publishers, 1998 for a comprehensive review of relevant topography.

📖 Chapter 3

Contextual Inquiry

Section three is the contextual inquiry and has three items of concern. Item one discovers the main speaker, teacher, preacher, writer and so forth. Item two discovers the authority claim, divine call or commission. Item three discovers to whom spoken, taught, preached, written and so forth.

Item one inquiry helps to discover whether the passage content is the words or deeds (a thing done; a brave, skillful or unusual act; or feat) of God, Satan, demons, angels or man. *Search Rule:* First look in the text, context and background for either the words or deeds – discovery should come in or before the text. When Scripture discovery is outside the background two references, such as, a proper name for example, "Jesus of Nazareth said" and a pronoun for example, "He said" are required. The inquiry about the *speaker* requires the discovery of the recorded sayings of the main character while ministering in public. Events surrounding the hustle and bustle of daily ministry, as is the case with Jesus of Nazareth are good examples. The inquiry about the *teacher* requires the discovery of the recorded sayings of the main character in confined places such as the temple, synagogue, and homes of friends or acquaintances. This is also true when the main character is in a seated position, for example, at supper or sitting on the mount. Pay close attention to scriptural reference about customs and traditions of the holy land. For example: *And he came to Nazareth, where he had been brought up; and as his custom was, he went into the synagogue on the Sabbath day, and stood up for to read (Luke 4:16).*

Contextual Inquiry

The inquiry about the *preacher* requires the discovery of the duration of the oratory. The Sermon on the Mount (Matthew 5:1 – 7:29) is an excellent example. Jesus sat on the mount to teach and because of the lengthy duration, his teaching is became a sermon. Inquires made of other main characters, other than Jesus of Nazareth are also found within the study passage. This also includes events, prayers, miracles, casting out demons and so forth. Continuing our example from our study passage, we discover that Jesus of Nazareth is teaching as recorded in (Matthew 13:1-3). This passage also uncovered three gems of truth. First, Jesus of Nazareth is the main character (Matthew 13:1). Second, Jesus sat by the seaside and later he went into a ship, and sat (Matthew 13:1, 2). The customs and tradition of the Holy lands, about a Rabbi, teacher or master sitting down to speak means a position of authority of the speaker. Jesus is teaching. In the circuit court of Leon County, Tallahassee, Florida, for example, the bailiff announces the honorable judge by name and jurisdiction. The judge sits down and the bailiff declares the court is now in session. This familiar practice of present-day courtroom decorum is a specter of ancient biblical customs and traditions. Third, the Holy Spirit reveals Jesus in Matthew's account as Jesus. In John's account, Jesus is Jesus of Nazareth (John 1:45). In the epistle, Jesus Christ gave Paul apostolic authority but Paul penned his letter to the church of God at Corinth sanctified by Christ Jesus (I Corinthians 1:1, 2). Who is Jesus, Jesus Christ, Christ Jesus or Jesus of Nazareth? What is the proper biblical reference for use in each study passage? This distinction is more than just other names for Christ or revelation of his character.

Contextual Inquiry

This distinction as used in scripture shows how the Holy Spirit reveals Jesus in various stages of his ministry. *First,* the revelation of Jesus as the Word is recorded in (John 1:1). This distinction marks his preexistence ministry (Genesis through Malachi). (Psalms 2:7) affirm this. Jesus preexistence confirmed during his earthly ministry (John 8:58) is proclaimed by the apostles to the church (Colossians 1:15-19).

Second, the revelation of Jesus as Jesus of Nazareth is recorded in (John 1:45). This distinction marks his incarnation ministry from (Matthew through John). This revelation revealed to Joseph in a dream *"and thou shall call his name JESUS." Behold, a virgin shall be with child and shall bring forth a son, and they shall call his name Emmanuel, which being interpreted is, God with us* (Matthew 1:21-23). *Third,* the revelation of Jesus as the Christ is recorded in (Matthew 28:9). This distinction marks his resurrection ministry for about forty days before his ascension when about four-hundred brethren saw him including Paul of Tarsus. *Fourth,* the revelation of Jesus as Christ Jesus is recorded in (1 Corinthians 1:2; Ephesians 1:1; and Philippians 1:1. This distinction marks his ascension ministry (Acts – Revelation) sitting on the right hand of God as our advocate with the Father. Even when the distinction is absent from the context of the study passage, the Holy Spirit reveals Jesus. This is significant when studying the four gospel accounts and epistles. **Item two** confirms any authority claims, divine call or commission and so forth. A prophet, for example, might carry more authority than that of a king or perhaps even a priest depending on the context. Jesus of Nazareth confirms only His claims as Emanuel.

Contextual Inquiry

Let us examine hierarchy authority claims made by Jesus of Nazareth during His earthly ministry.

Chart 4-4

JESUS HIERARCHY AUTHORITY CLAIMS
1. Jesus of Nazareth Asserts that He is God for example, Luke 4:8; 12
2. "I AM" Saying for example, John 15:1
3. TITLES 3.1 Son of God = Divine title 3.2 Son of David = Jewish title 3.3 Son of man = Earthly title
4. DIVINE ATTRIBUTES: 4.1 Omnipotent 4.2 Omniscience 4.3 Omnipresence

The discovery of the authority claim of Jesus for the kingdom parable in (Matthew 13:31, 32) requires going outside the background and quoting the nearest passage to the text. Jesus claim to be the "Son of Man," when He answered the scribes and the Pharisees question about signs. *For as Jonah was three days and three nights in the wale's belly; so shall the Son of man be three days and three nights in the heart of the earth* (Matthew 12:40). Everyone, including the author and readers of this publication must find scriptural support for our claim, call and commission. Paul, an apostle, for example, validates his claim, call and commission. He signed the letter to the Romans, as was routine for ancient letter writers. In it, he **claimed** to be an apostle. *Paul, a servant of Jesus Christ, called to be an apostle, and separated unto the gospel of God* (Romans 1:1). In addition, Paul's **divine call** as recorded by Luke in (Acts 9:1-31) confirms his ministry. Moreover, the discovery of Paul's **commission** also called his ordination took place at the local church in Antioch (Acts 13:1-4).

Contextual Inquiry

As they ministered to the Lord, and fasted, the Holy Ghost said, Separate me Barnabas and Saul for the work where unto I have called them (Acts 13:2). Finally, Jesus of Nazareth whose claims supported by His incarnation speaks with the authority of God with self-confirmation. We seek to discover the claim, call and commission of all other biblical characters mentioned in the study passage, as an integral part of the Dialectical Method's contextual inquiry. **Item three** discovers the audience or recipients taking part in the historic events with any recorded respond. The multitude is the audience for the kingdom parables based on Jesus circle of influence. *And great multitudes were gathered together unto him, so that he went into a ship, and sat; and the whole multitude stood on the shore* (Matthew 13:1). Chart 5-5

CIRCLES OF INFLUENCE
1. Jesus and John
2. Peter, James and John (Inner Circle)
3. The Twelve Apostles
4. Jesus Friends, Disciples, 120, 70, 400
5. The Multitude - Jews, Scribes, Publicans
6. Not Applicable

Also, Matthew records that Jesus sent the multitude away and went into the house with his disciples (Matthew 13:36) and continued teaching and providing interpretation until finishing the kingdom parable discourse. *And it came to pass, that when Jesus had finish these parables, he departed thence* (Matthew 13:53).

Though this is a change in the circle of influences from the multitude to the disciples, it does not affect the exegesis of any kingdom parable recorded in (Matthew 13:31b, 32).

Chapter 4

Applying Exegetical Methods

Section four applies the exegetical methods. Exegetical methods, namely, list, decode, narrative, epistle, miracle, prophetic and prayer exegesis are integral parts of the Dialectical Method. Each exegetical method designed to examine Scripture based on its form of composition is a work-in-progress. What is Exegesis? *The Dictionary of Christian Theology* defines it this way. The Greek verb behind this noun means to direct, to expound or interpret. (*Eisegesis*, a word sometimes used by way of contrast, would mean reading into a text instead of reading the meaning from it). In traditional usage hermeneutics lay down the general rules of interpretation (of Scripture, etc), while exegesis is concerned with their actual application to a given text. [1] Further, I embrace Bullinger's importance of Figurative Language that bring power and force to words. Bullinger states it this way. For an unusual form (*figura*) is never used except to *add* force to the truth, convey emphasis to the statement of it, and depth to the meaning of it. When we apply this science both to God's words and to divine truths, we see at once that no branch of Bible study can be more important, or offer greater promise of substantial reward. [2] The Dialectical Method draws from the Greek meaning of exegesis "to direct" as in the systematic and prayerful study of scripture while depending on the Holy Spirit to illuminate Bullinger's (*figura*) when found in the study passage. Continuing our example from Matthew's account of the parable (Matthew 13:1-3) and after checking Appendix II, p., 129, the decode exegesis is applicable for study of this parable.

Applying Exegetical Methods

Another parable put he forth unto them, saying, The <u>kingdom of heaven</u> is like to a grain of mustard seed, which a man took, and sowed in his field: Which indeed is the least of all seeds: but when it is grown, it is the greatest among herbs, and becometh a tree, so that the birds of the air come and lodge in the branches thereo (Matthew 13:31-32).

- Decode Exegesis

This method is only for poetry, such as, parables allegories and proverbs but works well with the Listing Exegesis when necessary. Let us examine parts of the decode method.

I.   **Thematic Statement** - often found at the beginning of the literary form may also appear outside the parable, proverb or allegory itself.

The kingdom of heaven (Matthew 13:31b) is the thematic statement (topic) of the parable. If the kingdom of heaven as the topic is the term *(figura)*, it needs defining or clarifying within the context of the passage. After checking both Holman Bible Dictionary and Willington Guide to the Bible, I embrace Dr. H. L Willmington's first meaning: The kingdom of heaven is the general rule of the Father from heaven over the affairs of men from creation to the millennium. Both saved and unsaved belongs to this kingdom. Christ had this general meaning in mind in Matthew 13. [3]

Bullinger explains the study passage *(figure)* known as Parcemia in this manner: "Like a grain of mustard seed" (Matthew 13:31, 32; 17:20, Luke 17:6). This was doubtless a proverbial saying among the Hebrews (not the Greeks), to indicate a very small thing: as we say, of rent, etc. [4]

Applying Exegetical Methods

II. **Illustrative Material** - Examples, illustrations, explanation, figure of speech used to "context" the theme or subject. Whatever makes it plain? Remember, some authors intentionally obscure parables, proverbs and allegories that make it difficult for the reader to extract understanding or meaning.

The definition is consistent with the *(Figura)* of the passage as Jesus uses a literary device known as a *simile* to explain the moral point. A short figure of comparison, a simile involves an explicit comparison of two unlike things using the words "as" or "like," for example, (Matthew 13:31b). [5]

III. **Moral Point** (Central Truth)

What is the Central Truth? The thematic statement (topic) of the parable is the *Kingdom of heaven* (Matthew 13:31b-32) and the rest of the parable is illustrative material based on figures of speech. What is the moral point? The moral point (central truth) is the kingdom parable in its entirety as explained by Jesus.

There are some parables that include an interpretation. In these instances the Decode Exegesis includes - **Thematic Statement, Illustrative Material, Interpretation,** and **Moral Point**. See the parable of the Sower (Matthew 13:3-9) and its accompanied interpretation (Matthew 13:18-23) and the parable of the Tares (Matthew 13:24-30) and its accompanied interpretation (Matthew 13:36-43). Also, see the list of kingdom parables from the four gospels Chart 6-6, page 38).

Applying Exegetical Methods

Chart 6-6

THE KINGDOM OF HEAVEN
1. Like a farmer, Matthew 13:24
2. Like a seed, Matthew 13:31
3. Like yeast, Matthew 13:33
4. Like treasure, Matthew 13:44
5. Like a pearl merchant, Matthew 13:45
6. Like a fishnet, Matthew 13:47
7. Like an employer, Matthew 20:1
8. Like a king inviting people to a marriage feast, Matthew 22:2
9. Like ten young women, Matthew 25:1
10. Glad tidings of the kingdom, Luke 8:1
11. Mystery of the Kingdom of God, Mark 4:11

Applying Exegetical Methods

Notes

1. Richardson Alan, editor, A *Dictionary of Christian Theology*, The Westminster Press, Philadelphia, 1967 p. 123.
The contributors to this Dictionary come from several different Christian traditions. While it is hoped that a high degree of objectivity preserved in matters of scholarship and verifiable historical fact, it is certain and indeed desirable that writers should present the subject from his own view, p. vi.

2. Bullinger E. W., *Figures of Speech Used in the Bible*, Baker Book House, Grand Rapids, Michigan, 1968, p. vi.
Jehovah has given us revelation of His mind and His will in words. It is therefore necessary that we should understand not merely the meanings of the words themselves, but also the laws, which govern their usage and combinations, p. v.

3. Willmington H. L., *Willmington's GUIDE to the BIBLE*, Tyndale House Publishers, Wheaton, Illinois, 1983 p. 295.

Definition of the Kingdom Of Heaven

First Meaning
The kingdom of heaven is the general rule of the Father from heaven over the affairs of men from creation to the millennium. Both saved and unsaved belong to this kingdom. (Daniel 4:17, 32; Matthew 8:12; 22:2; 25:1) Christ had this general meaning in mind in Matthew 13.

Applying Exegetical Methods

Second Meaning

The kingdom of heaven is that specific rule of the Son from Jerusalem over the affairs of men during the millennium. Only saved people will enter this kingdom (Matthew 6:10, 13; 25:34; 26:29).

4. Bullinger E. W., *Figures of Speech Used In the Bible*, Baker Book House, 1999 p. 758.

5. Boa Kenneth D, *The Open Bible Companion*, Thomas Nelson Publishers, 1986 p. 49.
This spiral-bound publication is the complete (out of print) guide to getting the most from your Open Bible for lesson, study, and sermons.

📖 Chapter 5

Exegetical Inquiry

Section five is the exegetical inquiry and has three items of inquiries. Item one discovers how we should accept this Scripture. Should we accept it literally or figuratively? Item two discovers how we discover its application. Scripture application is its literally fulfillment of Bible prophecy for one of the following: The Church, the World or Israel. Item three discovers how to decide its profitability: doctrine, reproof, correction or instruction in righteousness. Let us continue with an exegetical inquiry of the Kingdom parable beginning with the Text – (Matthew 13:31b, 32).

Item one – asks how should we accept the central truth of the passage either literal or figuratively? This question presumes the completed exegesis and the truth of God's word made known. The passage is regarded as literal. This infers to the help of the Holy Spirit to work through the *(figura)* of the passage for understanding its literal teaching.

Item two – asks how should we decide its application? God's Plan and Purpose for the Church, the World and Israel, spoken by the Major and Minor Prophets, consist of one fourth of all Scripture. Therefore, Scripture may be understood and fulfilled literally, considering, Bible prophecy for the Church, Israel or the World. Let us begin by examining four views of the church. *Holman Bible Dictionary* describes the church as a group of people claiming trust in Jesus Christ, meeting to worship Him, and seeking to enlist others to become His followers. [1]

Exegetical Inquiry

The Dictionary of Christian Theology describes church as the Body of Christ because its true nature rest on its relation to God's purpose. Understood this way the opposition between metaphor and non-metaphor are unreal. [2] R C Sproul describes the church as all the people who belong to the Lord and purchased by the blood of Christ. Various other images and expressions also define or describe the church. The church called the body of Christ, the people of God, the elect, the bride of Christ; the company of the redeemed; the communion of saints, the new Israel is among us. [3] Matthew records Jesus of Nazareth words to Peter: *And I say also unto thee, That thou art Peter, and upon this rock I will build my church; and the gates of hell shall not prevail against it* (Matthew 16:18). The biblical description of church helps clarify the Kingdom parables as taught by Jesus, which does not address issues related to the New Testament church. Jesus proclamation that *"I will build my church"* reveals His future relationship with believers rather than a physical building. Each of the four descriptions supports this conclusion. Scripture does not refer to the church as the kingdom of heaven. If the kingdom parable does not address church issues, does Jesus direct His teaching to the world? Let us begin by examining *Holman Bible Dictionary* description of the world. In the non-hostile sense world means the completely created order. Paul before the Areopagus in Athens spoke of the *God who made the world and everything in it*: (Acts 17:24). The hostile sense of "the world" revealed in the Johannine writings is self-evident. Nevertheless, the world is not inherently evil. John still affirms creation of the world through the *logos* (John 1:3-4). Since both, good and evil exist in the Kingdom of God. [4]

Exegetical Inquiry

Holman's description makes clear - the god of this world is Satan (1 John 4:4; 2 Corinthians 4:4). Therefore, the kingdom parables underline God's rule over the world even though Satan is its prince.

Applying the kingdom parables require that we understand that Israel are descendants of Jacob beginning as a nation in Egypt (Genesis 49:16, 28; Exodus 1:12, 20). Currently the World, the Church and Israel exist within an interconnected prophetic web of revelations specific to the destiny of each. The kingdom parables prove that God sits on the throne governing the world as explained by Jesus' variety of parable compositions. Therefore, this application of the kingdom parables makes it one of a Biblical principle. A principle that transcends, for example (Acts 10:43) the dispensation of the Old Testament and the New Testament.

Item three - how do we decide the kingdom parables profitability? Do the kingdom parables offer doctrine (teaching either truth or error), reproof (a cutting rebuke for misconduct), correction (punishment designed to restore) or instruction in righteousness (a lifestyle of uprightness before God) as displayed through faith and practice? Jesus, the Son of God, taught the kingdom parables as doctrinal truths of and about the God of creation (Genesis 1:1).

Exegetical Inquiry

Notes

1. *Holman Bible Dictionary*, Edited by Trent C. Butler, Holman Bible Publisher, Nashville, Tennessee, 1991. 843, p. 4.

2. *A Dictionary of Christian Theology*, Edited by Alan Richardson, The Westminster Press, Philadelphia, 1969, p. 65.

3. Sproul R. C., *Essential Truths of the Christian Faith*, Tyndale House Publishers, Wheaton Illinois, 1992, p. 217.

4. *Holman Bible Dictionary*, Edited by Trent C. Butler, Holman Bible Publisher, Nashville, Tennessee 1991, pp. 843, 1420.

Chapter 6

List Exegesis

Text - I Corinthians 9:2

SECTION ONE – Study Method

The Dialectical Method of Biblical Exegesis is a Revelation Paradigm for Students Taught by the Holy Spirit Studying Scripture.

SECTION TWO – Determining – Textual – Historical – Literary Context

Text – *If I be not an apostle unto others, yet doubtless I am to you: for the seal of mine apostleship are ye in the Lord* (I Corinthians 9:2). The text when put back into its context becomes the study passage.

Context – Using the outline taken from a Study Bible Edition of the *Authorized King James Version*, the context of the study passage is (I Corinthians 9:1-14). When studying an epistle, deciding its subject matter is pivotal in clarifying the study passage. Also, see background discussion, p., 47.

Literary Form – The literary form is an epistle. I agree with Kenneth D. Boa's explanation that epistles follow standard form of ancient letters. The form includes the name of the writer, the name of the recipient, a greeting, a wish or thanksgiving, the body of the letter, and final greeting and farewell. [1]

List Exegesis

Do not confuse figures of speech used by the writer to compose the epistle with that of literary forms. Literary forms found in Scripture include narrative, poetry, wisdom literature, prophetic literature, gospel, parable, epistle and so forth. Defining figures of speech as figurative expressions used to compose literary forms provides clarity to the difference. Examining figures of speech takes place in Section Four – applying exegetical methods.

Contextual Rules – Four rules governs valid reasons for going outside the study passage. (Please refer to definition on pp., 25 and 26). Let us examine three verses in the study passage under rule number one about the passage composition that uses citations, quotes, or application of revelation truth from prior passages. No other rules are applicable for this study passage. The (R superscription) above the passage marks a valid reference under rule one.

Who goeth a warfare any time at his own charges? who ^{R} planteth a vineyard, and eateth not of the fruit thereof? or who ^{R} feedeth a flock, and eateth not of the milk of the flock? (I Corinthians 9:7) 　　　　　　　　　Deuteronomy 20:6 * John 21:15

References Rule no. 1

And what man is he that hath planted a vineyard, and hath not yet eaten of it? let him also go and return unto his house, lest he die in the battle, and another man eat of it (Deuteronomy 20:6)

So when they had dined, Jesus saith to Simon Peter, Simon, son of Jonas, lovest thou me more than these? He saith unto him, Yea, Lord; thou knowest that I love thee. He saith unto him, Feed my lambs. (John 21:15)

List Exegesis

For it is written in the law of Moses, R Thou shalt not muzzle the mouth of the ox that treadeth out the corn. Doth God take care for oxen? (I Corinthians 9:9).   Deuteronomy 25:4

References Rule no 1

Thou shalt not muzzle the ox when he treadeth out the corn (Deuteronomy 25:4).

Even so hath the Lord ordained R that they which preach the gospel should live of the gospel   (I Corinthians 9:14).
Numbers 18:21

References rule no 1

And, behold, I have given the children of Levi all the tenth in Israel for an inheritance, for their service which they serve, even the service of the tabernacle of the congregation (Numbers 18:21).

Background – The background is (I Corinthians 9:1-27). Deciding topics or grouping of topics helps discover the epistle background. This includes broad themes or collection of themes rather than stages or settings where events took place. Settings, stages and events used for narratives with its applicable exegesis help discover the background. Paul explains his liberty by first listing his rights as a minister (1 – 14) and second by listing his rights for ministry (15 – 27). The overall theme or topic is Paul's defense of his apostleship. **Panoramic View** – Paul called to be an apostle of Jesus Christ is the writer of this epistle. Though his panoramic collections are many, only his two letters (II Corinthians & I) to the church of God at Corinth are applicable for our study passage. Also, if the study passage were (2 timothy 2:15, 16), the panoramic view becomes II Timothy & I. Additionally, if the study passage were (Romans 5:17), the panoramic view becomes the Epistle to the Romans.

List Exegesis

The minimum consideration for the panoramic view is the author and collection of literature. Topography, relevant responses and so forth are not applicable when studying an epistle. (See p., 29 for discussion of panoramic view).

SECTION THREE – Contextual Inquiry

Who is the main speaker, teacher, preacher writer or other?
- Paul called to be an apostle of Jesus Christ through the will of God is the letter writer.

Paul called to be an apostle of Jesus Christ through the will of God, and Sosthenes our brother (I Corinthians 1:1).

What is the authority: claims, divine call, commission or other?

Chart 7-7

WHO IS APOSTLE PAUL?
* *Paul's Claim* - Apostle (I Corinthians 1:1 or search at the beginning of each Epistle.) * *Paul's Call* - Paul experience on the Damascus road (Acts 9: 1-31) consists of his divine meeting with Jesus of Nazareth. * *Paul's Commission* - Paul was commission by the Holy Ghost at the local church in Antioch (Acts 13:1-4).

Who is the audience of the speaker, teacher, preacher, writer or other? Paul wrote this letter to the church of God, which is at Corinth.

List Exegesis

Unto the church of God which is at Corinth, to them that are sanctified in Christ Jesus, called to be saints, with all that in every place call upon the name of Jesus Christ our Lord, both their's and our's: (I Corinthians 1:2).

SECTION FOUR – Applying the Exegetical Methods

Discovering the Central Truth – Generally, the Epistle Exegesis would be the tool of choice for Paul's letter. This exegesis works best with formal epistles where the writer is addressing issues about what the assembly should believe or how the assembly should live. When the writer addresses problems, the Epistle Exegesis has the advantage. When problem do not exist and the writer exalts the believers to Christian virtue, the List Exegesis is the tool of choice. Dr. Kenneth D. Boa provides some insight into the spectrum of epistles. On one end of the spectrum of letters is the personal, nonliterary letter; on the other end is the formal epistle that is intended for the public and posterity. The epistles of the New Testament are unusual in that they combine elements of both. [2] The List Exegesis, however, is applicable for our study passage.

- Applying the List Exegesis

Part A: Listing is an investigative study of key words, phrases, verses, figures of speech, passages requiring explanation, definition or understanding within the passage. Look up the meaning in a Bible dictionary, book on literary forms, book of figure of speech and so forth. Please refer to Listing Exegesis Appendix III, p., 130.

List Exegesis

Book of 1 Corinthians, Chapter 9

9:1 *Am I not an apostle? am I not free? have I not seen Jesus Christ our Lord? are not ye my work in the Lord?*
Paul asked four rhetorical questions (questions ask only for effect and not for information.) He gives the answer in verse two.

9:2 *If I be not an apostle unto others, yet doubtless I am to you: for the seal of mine apostleship are ye in the Lord.*

9:3 *Mine answer to them that do examine me is this,*

Paul Outlines His Apostolic Defense 9:4 - 14

9:4 *Have we not power to eat and to drink?* [at the expenses of our converts or of the church] Without this, there is no sequence in the apostle's argument. Alternatively, we may supply [without working with our own hands]. Also, see verse 6 and 7. Ellipsis, the figure means some gap left in the sentence and a word or words are *left out or omitted*. The English name of, the figure would therefore be Omission. [3]

9:5 *Have we not power to lead about a sister, a wife, as well as other apostles, and as the brethren of the Lord, and Cephas?*

9:6 *Or I only and Barnabas, have not we power to forbear working?*

List Exegesis

9:7 *Who goeth a warfare any time at his own charges? who planteth a vineyard, and eateth not of the fruit thereof? or who feedeth a flock, and eateth not of the milk of the flock?* Parcemia is a figure for any sententious saying, because these are generally such as control and influence life. Also see Matthew 10:10; Luke 10:7 as examples of Parcemia "The workman is worthy of his meat." [4] Erotesis is important because this form of question conveys some of the weightiest truths. For example, where the question is put in the affirmative and the answer supplied by the mind is an emphatic negative. *"Who goeth a warfare any time at his own charges?"* [5]

9:8 *Say I these things as a man? or saith not the law the same also?*

9:9 *For it is written in the law of Moses, Thou shalt not muzzle the mouth of the ox that treadeth out the corn. Doth God take care for oxen?*

9:10 *Or saith he it altogether for our sakes? For our sakes, no doubt, this is written: that he that ploweth should plow in hope; and that he that thresheth in hope should be partaker of his hope.* Ellipsis – *"Doth God take care for oxen [only]? Or saith he it altogether for our sakes?"* [6]

9:11 *If we have sown unto you spiritual things, is it a great thing if we shall reap your carnal things?*

9:12 *If others be partakers of this power over you, are not we rather? Nevertheless we have not used this power; but suffer all things, lest we should hinder the gospel of Christ.*

9:13 *Do ye not know that they which minister about holy things live of the things of the temple? and they which wait at the altar are partakers with the altar?*

9:14 *Even so hath the Lord ordained that they which preach the gospel should live of the gospel.*

List Exegesis

Part B: The List or Listing Exegesis also refers to listings of gifts, sequence of commands, and order of covenants. Ask two questions for illumination:

1. Does the listing (The eleven points of Paul apostolic defense) reference a **[X]** hierarchical or [ ] lineal? Hierarchical means the first mentioning is of greater importance than the later. Lineal meaning that all items in the listing are of equal significance.
2. Does the listing reference an **[X]** inclusive listing or an [ ] exclusive listing? Inclusive means that other similar items added to the list makes the list open. Exclusive means a close listing, such as the Godhead: Father Son & Holy Spirit.

What is the Central Truth? - The List Exegesis (verse-by-verse examination) reveals the use of several figures of speech that add emphasis and depth of meaning. In addition, this portion of Paul's letter has two parts. The first part begins with a rhetorical question, for which Paul gives an answer: The second part list his apostolic defenses. The answer to Paul's rhetorical questions is the Central Truth.

If I be not an apostle unto others, yet doubtless I am to you: for the seal of mine apostleship are ye in the Lord. (I Corinthians 9:2).

List Exegesis

SECTION FIVE – Exegetical Inquiry

How should we accept this Scripture? Paul makes a literal statement in defense of his apostleship. Its purpose and meaning is clear and present-day readers should accept it as *literal*. How do we decide its application? The application examines as clear as possible the intent of the writer. The intended audience is the Church, World or Israel. Since Paul is addressing his letter to the *Church* of God at Corinth, the continuity of revelation makes his defense applicable today. How do we decide its profitability? Choose from doctrine, reproof, correction and instruction in righteousness. If Paul is an example, that believers must live *upright* before God as displayed through faith and practice two things are self-evident: Proof of Paul's apostolic appointment and his authority to set forth *instruction in righteousness.*

List Exegesis

Notes

1. Boa Kenneth D, *The Open Bible Companion*, Thomas Nelson Publishers, 1986, p.60. This spiral-bound publication is the complete (out of print) guide to getting the most from your Open Bible for lesson, study, and sermons.

2. *Ibid.*

3. Bullinger E. W., *Figures of Speech Used in the Bible*, Baker Book House, Grand Rapids, Michigan, 1968, pp.1, 51.

4. *Ibid.*, pp. 755, 763.

5. *Ibid.*, pp. 949, 950.

6. *Ibid.*, p. 24.

📖 Chapter 7

Decode Exegesis

Text – John 10:10

SECTION ONE – Study Method

The Dialectical Method of Biblical Exegesis is a Revelation Paradigm for Students Taught by the Holy Spirit Studying Scripture.

SECTION TWO – Determining – Textual – Historical – Literary Context

Text - *The thief cometh not, but for to steal, and to kill, and to destroy: I am come that they might have life, and that they might have it more abundantly* (John 10:10). The text when put back into its context becomes the study passage. **Context** – Using the outline taken from a Study Bible Edition of the *Authorized King James Version*, the study passage is (John 10: 1-21). When studying a parable, extended figures of speech are pivotal in clarifying the study passage. **Literary Form** – The literary form is a parable. I agree with Kenneth Boa's explanation that parables are figures of comparison that often use short stories to teach a truth or answer a question. While the story in a parable is not historical, it is true to life, not a fairy tale. As a form of oral literature, the parable exploits realistic situations but makes effective use of imagination. [1] Jesus composed parables using natural and common situations known to the hearer to draw a corresponding spiritual truth. Please refer to Appendix II Literary Forms Quick Chart p., 129.

Decode Exegesis

Contextual Rules - Four rules governs valid reasons for going outside the study passage. (For definition of valid rules, please refer to pp., 25 - 26). Let us examine four verses in the study passage under rule one about the passage composition that uses citations, quotes, or application of revelation truth from prior passages. No other rules are applicable for this study passage. The (R superscription) above the passage marks a valid reference under rule one.

I am the good [R] *shepherd, and know my sheep, and am known of mine* (John 10:14).   Isaiah 40:11
Verse 14 quotes from Isaiah 40:11 with the prophecy fulfilled in Luke 4:18f.

And [R] *other sheep I have, which are not of this fold: them also I must bring, and they shall hear my voice; and there shall be one fold, and one shepherd* (John 10:16).   Isaiah 42:6; 56:8
Verse 16 quotes from Isaiah 42:6, 56:8 with the prophecy fulfilled in Acts 10:45.

Therefore doth my Father love me, [R] *because I lay down my life, that I might take it again* (John 10:17).   Isaiah 53:7, 8, 12
Verse 17 quotes from Isaiah 53:7; 8, 12 with the prophecy fulfilled in John Chapter 20.

Others said, These are not the words of him that hath a devil. [R] *Can a devil open the eyes of the blind?* (John 10:21).
Exodus 4:11
Verse 21 quotes from Exodus 4:11 (Truth about the omnipotent God of Creation).

Decode Exegesis

Background – The background found in (John 8:1 - 10:21) gives us the stage or setting in which the event took place. Look for such events as the changing from one location to another, or giving a revelation to more than one group and changing subject matter. Check the outline in a Study Bible Edition of the *Authorized King James Version*. John records events in sequence beginning with events taking place after Jesus had attended the Feast of the Tabernacle. They include the woman caught in adultery, an announcement that He is the Light of the World, healing of the blind man and an announcement that He is the Good Shepherd.

Panoramic View – The panoramic view is the (Book of John, I, II and III Epistle and Book of Revelation). The panoramic view verifies the author, collection of literature, theological themes, custom and traditions of the Holy lands, first response of the hearers and relevant topography. Also, see Laney Carl J, *Concise Bible Atlas: A Geographical Survey of Bible History*, Hendrickson Publishers, 1998 for relevant topography.

SECTION THREE – Contextual Inquiry

Who is the main speaker, teacher, preacher writer or other? Jesus of Nazareth is speaking as recorded in John 10:7. *Search Rule:* First look in the text, context and background - validation should come in or before the text.

Then said Jesus unto them again, Verily, verily, I say unto you, I am the door of the sheep (John 10:7).

Decode Exegesis

What is the authority: claims, divine call, commission or other? Jesus announces that He is both the Door and the Good Shepherd according to John 10:7, 11.

I am the good shepherd: the good shepherd giveth his life for the sheep (John 10:11).

John's account presents the most powerful case in the entire Bible for the deity of the incarnate Son of God. The deity of Jesus of Nazareth as revealed in His seven "I am" sayings.

Chart 8-8

JESUS "I AM" SAYINGS
1. I am the bread of life (John 6:35, 48)
2. I am the light of the world (John 8:12; 9:5)
3. I am the door (John 10:7, 9); I am the good shepherd (John 10:11, 14)
4. I am the resurrection and the life (John 11:25)
5. I am the way, the truth, and the life (John 14:6) and I am the true vine (John 15:1-5).

Who is the audience of the speaker, teacher, preacher, writer or other? Jesus though speaking to the Pharisees, His circle of influence represents the multitude. Also, see chart No. 5-5 the Circles of Influence of Jesus of Nazareth, on p., 34.

And some of the Pharisees which were with him heard these words, and said unto him, Are we blind also? (John 9:40).

Decode Exegesis

SECTION FOUR – Applying the Exegetical Methods

- Discovering the Central Truth

The Decode Exegesis is the tool of choice. It works best for wisdom literature, including psalms, allegories, parables, and similitudes which are all similar. Please refer to Decode Exegesis Appendix III, p., 131.

Book of John, Chapter 10

10:1 *Verily, verily, I say unto you, He that entereth not by the door into the sheepfold, but climbeth up some other way, the same is a thief and a robber.* Repetition means emphasis gained by techniques that repeat the same word, phrase, or sentence as shown in (v. 1a). [2] Parechesis is the repetition of words similar in sound, but different in language because they exist in another language and not in the translation of it (v. 1b). [3]

10:2 *But he that entereth in by the door is the shepherd of the sheep.*

10:3 *To him the porter openeth; and the sheep hear his voice: and he calleth his own sheep by name, and leadeth them out.*

10:4 *And when he putteth forth his own sheep, he goeth before them, and the sheep follow him: for they know his voice.*

10:5 *And a stranger will they not follow, but will flee from him: for they know not the voice of strangers.* Repeated Negation – It is a special form of *Synonymia*, the synonyms being negatives of different kinds heaped together for a special purpose. Negatives repeated in English strengthen and increase the emphasis: just as we say "no, no," "No, I will not." But in the Greek, this is done much more emphatically. [4]

Decode Exegesis

10:6 *This parable spake Jesus unto them: but they understood not what things they were which he spake unto them.*

10:7 *Then said Jesus unto them again, Verily, verily, I say unto you, I am the door of the sheep.*

10:8 *All that ever came before me are thieves and robbers: but the sheep did not hear them.* Synecdoche' of the GENUS is where the genus is put for the species; or universals for particulars. For example, all is put for the greater part: "All that ever came before me ..." [5] See verse 1.

10:9 *I am the door: by me if any man enter in, he shall be saved, and shall go in and out, and find pasture.* Synecdoche' of the Species – This is when the Species is put for the Genus (the opposite of the above), or when particulars are put for universals. For example, to go out and come in is used of official actions or of life in general (verse 9). [6]

10:10 *The thief cometh not, but for to steal, and to kill, and to destroy: I am come that they might have life, and that they might have it more abundantly.*

10:11 *I am the good shepherd: the good shepherd giveth his life for the sheep.* Anthropopatheia – This figure used of the ascription of human passions, actions, or attributes referring to God, for example, as the good shepherd (verse 11). [7]

10:12 *But he that is an hireling, and not the shepherd, whose own the sheep are not, seeth the wolf coming, and leaveth the sheep, and fleeth: and the wolf catcheth them, and scattereth the sheep.*

10:13 *The hireling fleeth, because he is an hireling, and careth not for the sheep.*

10:14 *I am the good shepherd, and know my sheep, and am known of mine.*

10:15 *As the Father knoweth me, even so know I the Father: and I lay down my life for the sheep.*

10:16 *And other sheep I have, which are not of this fold: them also I must bring, and they shall hear my voice; and there shall be one fold, and one shepherd.* Ampliatio – an old name for a new thing, such as, retaining of an old name after the reason for it is passed away. . "Other sheep I have" for example are so called, though they were not yet in existence, except in the purpose of the Father. [8]

10:17 *Therefore doth my Father love me, because I lay down my life, that I might take it again.* Heterosis (Of Tenses) – As the Hebrew verb has only two principal tenses, the past and the future, these two with the participles supply all the other tenses. These points out the present for the Paulo post *futurum* (This tense differs from the simple or perfect future by denoting and referring to something that will soon be past, verse 17). Also, to this first species of Metonymy must refer the use of the word SOUL for life, which is the effect of it. [9]

10:18 *No man taketh it from me, but I lay it down of myself. I have power to lay it down, and I have power to take it again. This commandment have I received of my Father.* Heterosis (Of Tenses) - The Present for the Future tense is put when the design is to show that some thing will happen, and is spoken of as though it were already present. [10]

Decode Exegesis

10:19 *There was a division therefore again among the Jews for these sayings.*

10:20 *And many of them said, He hath a devil, and is mad; why hear ye him?*

10:21 *Others said, These are not the words of him that hath a devil. Can a devil open the eyes of the blind?*

- Applying the Decode Exegesis

This method is only for poetry, such as, parable allegories and proverbs works well with the Listing Exegesis when necessary.

1. **Thematic Statement** - This is at the beginning of the literary form but sometimes outside the parable, proverb or allegory itself. THEME: *"But he that entereth in by the door is the shepherd of the sheep* (John 10:2). The shepherd represents Jesus of Nazareth and the sheep represent both Israel and the Church.

2. **Illustrative Material** - Examples, illustrations, explanation, figure of speech used to "context" the theme or subject. Making it plain is the important point. Remember, when an author obscure parables, or allegories with details or examples, they are without clarity of understanding. *Illustrative Material* – The illustrative portion found in (10:1, 3-5; 8; 10; 12-13; 15-21) which reflects the figures of speech contained in them. In addition, the three "I am" saying recorded in (John 10:9, 11, 14) require further study to discover the central truth.

Decode Exegesis

3. Moral Point (Central Truth)

Note: Jesus of Nazareth sometimes gives His parables an interpretation. When this is the case, the extended decode exegesis includes - Thematic Statement, Illustrative Material, Interpretation, and Moral Point.

What is the Central Truth? Jesus declared the prophets predicted the way in which the Messiah would come. Jesus gives the reference to the way the Messiah would come as the door (John 10:2). For example, the Messiah would come down through forty-two generation from the Tribe of Judah and blood heir to the Throne of David. The central truth is a declaration that Jesus is that door (John 10:9).

SECTION FIVE – Exegetical Inquiry

How should we accept this Scripture? Jesus announced, "I am the door." Its meaning is figurative yet clear. All present-day Bible readers should accept it as *literal*. How do we decide its application? Discover the application by examining as clear as possible the intent of this saying. The use of figures of speech draws emphasis to the declaration about both the Church and Israel. When the teaching transcends dispensational theology, it is clearly a Biblical *principle*. How do we decide its profitability? Choose from doctrine, reproof, correction and instruction in righteousness. Jesus establishes *doctrine* about the purpose of God and His ministry.

Notes

1. Boa Kenneth D, *The Open Bible Companion*, Thomas Nelson Publishers, 1986, p. 53.

2. *Ibid.*, p. 52.

3. Bullinger E. W., *Figures of Speech Used in the Bible*, Baker Book House, Grand Rapids, Michigan, 1968, pp. 321, 322.

4. *Ibid.*, p. 339.

5. *Ibid.*, pp. 614, 615.

6. *Ibid.*, pp. 623, 630.

7. *Ibid.*, pp. 872, 891.

8. *Ibid.*, pp. 689, 690.

9. *Ibid.*, pp. 517, 522, 544.

10. *Ibid.*, pp. 521, 522.

Chapter 8

Narrative Exegesis

Text – Genesis 18:25

SECTION ONE – Study Method

The Dialectical Method of Biblical Exegesis is a Revelation Paradigm for Students Taught by the Holy Spirit Studying Scripture.

SECTION TWO – Determining – Textual – Historical – Literary Context

Text - *That be far from thee to do after this manner, to slay the righteous with the wicked: and that the righteous should be as the wicked, that be far from thee: Shall not the Judge of all the earth do right?* **(Genesis 18:25).** The text when put back into its context becomes the study passage.

Context – Using the outline taken from an *Authorized King James Version* Study Bible, the study passage is (Genesis 18:16-33). Studying historical narratives requires an examination of the sovereignty of God. Understanding God's sovereignty over individuals and places is essential for clarifying the study passage.

Literary Form – The literary form is a historical narrative. The narrative is historical because it contains proper names of real people, places or things. The most common literary form in the Bible is a narrative. Narratives consist of a theme of subject matter, story plot, events, questions and answers and unfolding dramas. Please refer to Appendix II Literary Forms Quick Chart p., 129.

Narrative Exegesis

Contextual Rules - Four rules governs valid reasons for going outside the study passage. (For discussion on valid rules, please refer to pp., 25 and 26). Contextual rules are not applicable for this study passage. **Background** – The background found in (Genesis 18:1 - 20:18) gives us the stage or setting in which the event took place. Look for such events as the changing from one location to another, or giving a revelation to more than one group or changing subject matter. Check the outline in a Study Bible Edition of the *Authorized King James Version*. Genesis records events in sequence beginning with Sarah, Abraham wife, test of faith, next Abraham's test of faith and the final destruction of Sodom and Gomorrah. The background concludes with Lot's sin and the test of Abimelech. The study passage is about events, which test the covenant. **Panoramic View** – The panoramic view is the Pentateuch: (the book of Genesis, Exodus, Leviticus, Numbers, and Deuteronomy) Moses is the author. The panoramic view verifies the author, collection of literature, theological themes, customs and traditions of the Holy lands, first response of the hearers and relevant topography. Laney Carl J, *Concise Bible Atlas: A Geographical Survey of Bible History*, summarized the local region during this time. After separating from Lot, Abraham settled at "the oaks of Mamre." This later became know as Hebron (Genesis 13:18). His kinsman Lot's choice of the "well watered" valley of the Jordan is a bit problematic because of the present conditions of this region. Nevertheless, the biblical text acknowledges that this region was like "the garden of the LORD ... before the LORD destroyed Sodom and Gomorrah (Genesis 13:10)." It appears that some major geographical changes took place because of God's judgment on those evil cities.
1

Narrative Exegesis

SECTION THREE – Contextual Inquiry

Who is the main speaker, teacher, preacher writer or other? Genesis records a dialogue between Abraham and the Lord
Abraham is speaking (Genesis 18:16; 23) and the Lord is speaking (Genesis 18:17; 20). *Search Rule:* First look in the text, context and background - validation should come in or before the text.

And the LORD said, Shall I hide from Abraham that thing which I do (Genesis 18:17).

And Abraham drew near, and said, Wilt thou also destroy the righteous with the wicked? (Genesis 18:23).

What is the authority: claims, divine call, commission or other? Abraham had covenant authority with the Lord according to Genesis 12:1-3, Genesis 18:1. The God of creation (Genesis 1) set up both the Abrahamic Covenant and the first contact with Abraham. These make up Abraham's covenant authority.

Now the LORD had said unto Abram, Get thee out of thy country, and from thy kindred, and from thy father's house, unto a land that I will shew thee:
And I will make of thee a great nation, and I will bless thee, and make thy name great; and thou shalt be a blessing:
And I will bless them that bless thee, and curse him that curseth thee: and in thee shall all families of the earth be blessed. (Genesis 12:1-3).

Narrative Exegesis

And the LORD appeared unto him in the plains of Mamre: and he sat in the tent door in the heat of the day (Genesis 18:1).

Who is the audience of the speaker, teacher, preacher, writer or other? The dialogue is between Abraham and the Lord.

Chart 9-9

ABRAHAM TALKS WITH GOD	
ABRAHAM	THE LORD
Genesis • 18:23-25 • 27-28a • 29a • 30a • 31a • 32a	*Genesis* • 18:17-21 • 26 • 28b • 29b • 30b • 31b • 32b

Narrative Exegesis

SECTION FOUR – Applying the Exegetical Methods

- Discovering the Central Truth

The Narrative Exegesis is the tool of choice. It works best with narratives even when they contain special features, such as miracles, prophecy or major figures of speech. Some passages require the combining of exegetical methods because of complexity. Please refer to Narrative Exegesis Appendix III, p., 132.

Book of Genesis, Chapter 18

18:16
> *And the men rose up from thence, and looked toward Sodom: and Abraham went with them to bring them on the way.*

18:17
> *And the LORD said, Shall I hide from Abraham that thing which I do;* Erotesis (In Affirmative Negation) – The figure is used when a speaker or writer asks animated questions, but not to obtain information. In affirmative negation is important because this form of question conveys some of the weightiest truths: for example, where the question is put in the affirmative and the answer supplied by the mind is an emphatic negative. [1]

Narrative Exegesis

18:18

Seeing that Abraham shall surely become a great and mighty nation, and all the nations of the earth shall be blessed in him? Metonymy (Of Cause) is a figure by which one name or noun is used instead of another, to which it stands in a certain relation. Abraham is put for Christ by the same figure of Metonymy, "In thee shall all families of the earth be blessed: For another example, please refer to Galatians 13:3, p. 81. [3]

18:19

For I know him, that he will command his children and his household after him, and they shall keep the way of the LORD, to do justice and judgment; that the LORD may bring upon Abraham that which he hath spoken of him.

18:20

And the LORD said, Because the cry of Sodom and Gomorrah is great, and because their sin is very grievous; Prosopopceia - A figure by which things are represented or spoken of as persons; or, by which we attribute intelligence, by words or actions, to inanimate objects or abstract ideas. "The cry of Sodom and Gomorrah is great." This is Prosopopceia, whereas in James 5:4 we have it literally. [4]

18:21

I will go down now, and see whether they have done altogether according to the cry of it, which is come unto me; and if not, I will know. Anthropopatheia - Please refer to John 10:11 p., 60). [5]

Narrative Exegesis

18:22

And the men turned their faces from thence, and went toward Sodom: but Abraham stood yet before the LORD. Anthropopatheia – (Please refer to John 10:11 p., 60). [6]

18:23

And Abraham drew near, and said, Wilt thou also destroy the righteous with the wicked?

18:24

Peradventure there be fifty righteous within the city: wilt thou also destroy and not spare the place for the fifty righteous that are therein?

18:25

That be far from thee to do after this manner, to slay the righteous with the wicked: and that the righteous should be as the wicked, that be far from thee: Shall not the Judge of all the earth do right? Metonymy (Of Subject) is the land or earth is put for its inhabitants. (Please refer to Genesis 18:18 p., 70). [7]

18:26

And the LORD said, If I find in Sodom fifty righteous within the city, then I will spare all the place for their sakes.

18:27

And Abraham answered and said, Behold now, I have taken upon me to speak unto the LORD, which am but dust and ashes: Meiosis Or a be-littleing figure of one thing that diminishes to increase another thing. [8] Syntheton places together of two words by uses, for example, "dust and ash." [9]

Narrative Exegesis

18:28

Peradventure there shall lack five of the fifty righteous: wilt thou destroy all the city for lack of five? And he said, If I find there forty and five, I will not destroy it.

18:29

And he spake unto him yet again, and said, Peradventure there shall be forty found there. And he said, I will not do it for forty's sake.

18:30

And he said unto him, Oh let not the LORD be angry, and I will speak: Peradventure there shall thirty be found there. And he said, I will not do it, if I find thirty there.

18:31

And he said, Behold now, I have taken upon me to speak unto the LORD: Peradventure there shall be twenty found there. And he said, I will not destroy it for twenty's sake.

18:32

And he said, Oh let not the LORD be angry, and I will speak yet but this once: Peradventure ten shall be found there. And he said, I will not destroy it for ten's sake.

18:33

And the LORD went his way, as soon as he had left communing with Abraham: and Abraham returned unto his place.

Narrative Exegesis

- Applying the Narrative Exegesis

This narrative exegesis works with the List Exegesis, when examining figures of speech. There are four parts and one narrative question used with the narrative exegesis. You need to be able to identify each of these components should they exist in the narrative and are essential for revelation knowledge.

1. **Subject/Theme** - "And the Lord said, shall I hide from Abraham that thing which I do .. v. 17"
2. **Sequence of Events** – None
3. **Dialogue, Discussion, Questions & Answers** -

Dialogue

The Lord	**Genesis 18:17-21**
Abraham	Genesis 18:23-25
The Lord	**Genesis 18:26**
Abraham	Genesis 27-28a
The Lord	**Genesis 28b**
Abraham	Genesis 29a
The Lord	**Genesis 29b**
Abraham	Genesis 30a
The Lord	**Genesis 30b**
Abraham	Genesis 31a
The Lord	**Genesis 31b**
Abraham	Genesis 32a
The Lord	**Genesis 32b**

Question: What leads us to the central truth? Is it the subject or theme, sequence of events or dialogue? The dialogue leads us to the central truth.

Narrative Exegesis

4. What is the Central Truth? The Central Truth contained in Moses question about the Lord's Attribute as recorded in (Genesis 18:25). The Lord's answer implies that the cities met destruction because of fewer than ten righteous individuals.

Chart 10-2

NARRATIVE TYPES
Creation and Consummation – There are a remarkable number of parallels between the first and last three chapters of the Bible. *Epic* – An epic is a long narrative, often written in a lofty poetic style that combines many episodes. *Law* – A good portion of the narrative in Exodus 20 through Deuteronomy 31 written in the form of legislation for the nation of Israel is the basis for its legal system. *Heroic Narrative* – In this form of narrative literature, the story based on the exploits of the principal character make up the plot. *Tragedy* – Some of the protagonists of Scripture fell from a position of blessing to calamity. [10]

Chart compiled from -- Boa Kenneth, *The Open Bible Companion*, Thomas Nelson Publishers, 1986.

NOTES:
Historical narratives develop its plots with proper names including towns, cities as it unfolds its drama. The "Raising of Lazarus" from the dead is a good example. A special feature requires combining exegetical methods.

Narrative Exegesis

SECTION FIVE – Exegetical Inquiry

How should we accept this Scripture? The Lord's answer is *literal*. The cities met destruction because of fewer than ten righteous individuals. How do we decide its application? Discover the application by examining as clear as possible the intent of the dialogue between Abraham and the Lord. The intent of the Lord points to a truth that transcends the dispensation theology of the Old Testament and the New Testament, for example, Acts 10:43. When this is the case, it is a *biblical principle*. How do we decide its profitability? Choose from doctrine, reproof, correction and instruction in righteousness. The Lords' attributes – *"Shall not the Judge of all the earth do right?"* This is a *doctrine* statement about the sovereignty of God and His revealed justice.

Narrative Exegesis

Notes

1. Laney J Carl, *Concise Bible Atlas: A Geographical Survey of Bible History*, Hendrickson Publishers, 1999, p. 36.
Why study Biblical geography? *First,* a basic knowledge of the physical and climatic features of the land is necessary for a proper intellectual understanding of the Bible's narrative. *Second,* geography – by providing a rich and decorative backdrop for the dramatic events of biblical history – heightens the sensory and emotional impact of the narrative. *Third,* familiarity with biblical geography is important for one's theological view. *Fourth,* the study of biblical geography has an important relevance to teaching of Scripture, pp. 12-14.

2. Bullinger E. W., *Figures of Speech Used in the Bible*, Baker Book House, Grand Rapids, Michigan, 1968, pp. 943, 949.

3. *Ibid.*, pp. 538, 544.

4. *Ibid.*, pp. 861, 869.

5. *Ibid.*, p. 883.

6. *Ibid.*, p. 888.

7. *Ibid.*, p. 578.

8. *Ibid.*, p. 155.

9. *Ibid.*, p. 442.

10. *Ibid.*, pp. 55, 56.

📖 Chapter 9

Epistle Exegesis

Text – Galatians 3:10-14

> **SECTION ONE – *Study Method***

The Dialectical Method of Biblical Exegesis is a Revelation Paradigm for Students Taught by the Holy Spirit Studying Scripture.

> **SECTION TWO – Determining – Textual – Historical – Literary Context**

Text – Galatians 3:10- 14

3:11

For as many as are of the works of the law are under the curse: for it is written, Cursed is every one that continueth not in all things which are written in the book of the law to do them.

3:11

But that no man is justified by the law in the sight of God, it is evident: for, The just shall live by faith.

3:12

And the law is not of faith: but, The man that doeth them shall live in them.

3:13

Christ hath redeemed us from the curse of the law, being made a curse for us: for it is written, Cursed is every one that hangeth on a tree:

3:14

That the blessing of Abraham might come on the Gentiles through Jesus Christ; that we might receive the promise of the Spirit through faith.

Epistle Exegesis

The text when put back into its context becomes the study passage.

Context – Using the outline taken from a Study Bible Edition of the *Authorized King James Version*, the study passage is the same as the text (Galatians 3:10-14). When studying an epistle keep in mind Dr. Kenneth Boa understands that epistles exist on a spectrum. On one end of the spectrum of letters is the personal nonliterary letter; on the other end is the formal epistle that is intended for public consumption. [1]

Literary Form – The literary form is a formal epistle. Please refer to Appendix II Literary Forms Quick Chart p., 129.

Contextual Rules - Four rules governs valid reasons for going outside the study passage. (For discussion on valid rules, refer to pp., 25 and 26). Let us examine four verses in the study passage under rule one about the passage composition that uses citations, quotes, or application of revelation truth from prior passages. No other rules are applicable for this study passage. The (R superscription) above the passage marks a valid reference under rule one.

Galatians 3:10- 14

3:10
> For as many as are of the works of the law are under the curse: for it is written, [R] Cursed is every one that continueth not in all things which are written in the book of the law to do them. Verse 10 is a quote from Deuteronomy 27:26.

Epistle Exegesis

3:11

But that no man is justified by the law in the sight of God, it is evident: for, ^R The just shall live by faith. Verse 11 is a quote from Habakkuk 2:4.

3:13

Christ hath redeemed us from the curse of the law, being made a curse for us: for it is written, ^R Cursed is every one that hangeth on a tree: Verse 13 is a quote from Deuteronomy 21:23

3:14

That the blessing of Abraham might come on the Gentiles through Jesus Christ; that we might receive ^R the promise of the Spirit through faith. Verse 14 is a quote from Isaiah 49:6

Background – The background found in (Galatians 3:10-4:11) gives us the stage or setting in which the event took place. The Galatians, having begun their Christian experience by faith, seem content to leave their walk of faith and seek new principles based on works. Paul finds the paradigm shift intolerable. The epistles are topical and grouped around common themes. Check the outline in a Study Bible Edition of the *Authorized King James Version*. Paul addresses four topics in this section. First, Christ hath redeemed us from the curse of the law. Second, the law does not void the Abrahamic Covenant. Third, the laws given that drive us to faith come from God. Fourth, believers are free from the law.

Epistle Exegesis

Panoramic View – The panoramic view is the (Book of Galatians). The panoramic view verifies the author, collection of literature, theological themes, custom and traditions of the Holy lands, first response of the hearers and relevant topography. Laney Carl J, *Concise Bible Atlas: A Geographical Survey of Bible History* records that Paul busily engaged in ministry following his return from Asia Minor wrote the Epistle of Galatians in (A.D, 49). This letter sent to the recently established churches to underline the faith principle over and against legalistic Judaism. 2

SECTION THREE – Contextual Inquiry

Who is the main speaker, teacher, preacher writer or other? Paul is the writer as recorded in Galatians 1:1. *Search Rule:* First look in the text, context and background - validation should come in or before the text.

Paul, an apostle (not of men, neither by man, but by Jesus Christ, and God the Father, who raised him from the dead) (Galatians 1:1).

What is the authority: claims, divine call, commission or other? Paul is an Apostle. Please refer to Chart 7-7 page 48. Who is the audience of the speaker, teacher, preacher, writer or other? Paul writes to the Churches of Galatia (Galatians 1:2). In the New Testament, the term church from the Greek translates as assembly rather than "building". Paul is writing to the born-again, baptized believers in Christ Jesus, who live in Galatia.

And all the brethren which are with me, unto the churches of Galatia (Galatians 1:2).

Epistle Exegesis

SECTION FOUR – Applying the Exegetical Methods

- Discovering the Central Truth

The Epistle Exegesis is the tool of choice. Please refer to Epistle Exegesis Appendix III, p., 133.

Book of Galatians, Chapter 3

3:10 *For as many as are of the works of the law are under the curse: for it is written, Cursed is every one that continueth not in all things which are written in the book of the law to do them.*

3:11 *But that no man is justified by the law in the sight of God, it is evident: for, The just shall live by faith.*

3:12 *And the law is not of faith: but, The man that doeth them shall live in them.*

3:13 *Christ hath redeemed us from the curse of the law, being made a curse for us: for it is written, Cursed is every one that hangeth on a tree:* Metonymy (Of Cause) – Please refer to Genesis 18:18 p., 70. [3] Metonymy (Of The Adjunct) indicates that which is an accident, or belong to anything, is put for the subject or the thing itself to which it belongs. [4]

3:14 *That the blessing of Abraham might come on the Gentiles through Jesus Christ; that we might receive the promise of the Spirit through faith.* Antiptosis is a figure because one case is put instead of another case. *"The promise of the Spirit"* means the promised Spirit.

Epistle Exegesis

- Epistles Exegesis

STEP ONE – Discover the correct major thematic classifications:

> [X] The major thematic classification addresses revelation knowledge about what believers should believe. The doctrine of faith is a good example.
>
> [ ] The major thematic classification addresses revelation knowledge about how believers should live.

STEP TWO: Discover the correct major thematic constructions:

> [X] Declarative: Paul declares, for example, ye are *"Redeemed from the curse of the Law* (Galatians 3:13)"
>
> [ ] Descriptive: "We are of God little children and have overcome the world, for greater is he that is in me than he that is in the world.
>
> [ ] Conditional Descriptive: "If any man be in Christ, he is a new creature…"
>
> [ ] Prescriptive: "Walk in the Spirit and ye shall not fulfill the Lust of the flesh"

Epistle Exegesis

STEP THREE – Discover the applicable "P"

[X] Problem - The problem is more than statements or sequence of events. It has to do with the classical struggle that exist between good and evil. The battleground is the "Soul." Paul addresses the problem as - *"Under the curse of the Law, Galatians 3:10."*

[X] Principle – The principle is always the responsible of the individual with the problem with the help of the Holy Spirit (Acts 2:38). For example, discover the biblical principle that is violated thus causing the problem. Paul addresses the principle as - *"Christ hath redeemed from the curse of the Law, Galatians 3:13."*

[X] Promise – What saith the Scripture, how readest thou (Luke 10:26)? Paul addresses the promise as - *"Blessing of Abraham must come to the Gentiles, Galatians 3:14a."*

[X] Provision – The gospel of Christ is the power of God. This power breaks down deeply ingrained patterns of old lifestyles and replaces them with new lifestyles. This salvation is to everyone that believeth (Romans 1:16). Paul addresses the provision as - *"We might receive the promise of the Spirit through faith, Galatians 3:14b."*

What is the Central Truth? The central truth is (Galatians 3:13). When using the epistle exegesis and you discovers the principle, you have discovered the central truth. Paul states the problem as *"Under the curse of the Law, Galatians 3:10."* The only way to break this curse is to embrace *"Christ* [who] *hath redeemed* [us] *from the curse of the Law, Galatians 3:13."*

Epistle Exegesis

Notes: When the Epistle does not contain a problem, look for an exhortation of Christian virtue before abandoning the Epistle Exegesis. This exhortation often is the Central Truth. The nonliterary epistle uses the List Exegesis and the formal epistles use the Epistle Exegesis. Because of the Epistle spectrum, this exegesis is a work-in-progress.

SECTION FIVE – Exegetical Inquiry

How should we accept this Scripture? Paul writes *"Christ hath redeemed from the curse of the Law, Galatians 3:13."* Its meaning is exclusive yet clear. All present-day Bible readers should accept it as *literal*. How do we decide its application? Discover the application by examining as clear as possible the intent of the letter. Paul declares redemption for all who accept Christ and are no longer under the curse of the law. When the teaching transcends dispensational theology, it is clearly a Biblical *principle*. How do we decide its profitability? Choose from doctrine, reproof, correction and instruction in righteousness. Paul proves freedom from the law through redemption by Christ is *doctrinal*.

Notes

1. Boa Kenneth D, *The Open Bible Companion*, Thomas Nelson Publishers, 1986: p. 60.

2. Laney Carl J, *Concise Bible Atlas: A Geographical Survey of Bible History*, Hendrickson Publishers, 1998, p. 226.

3. Bullinger E. W., *Figures of Speech Used in the Bible*, Baker Book House, Grand Rapids, Michigan, 1968, p. 559.

Ibid., pp. 587, 591.

📖 Chapter 10

Miracle Exegesis

Text – John 2:11

> **SECTION ONE** – *Study Method*

The Dialectical Method of Biblical Exegesis is a Revelation Paradigm for Students Taught by the Holy Spirit Studying Scripture.

> **SECTION TWO** – Determining – Textual – Historical – Literary Context

Text – John 2:11

This beginning of miracles did Jesus in Cana of Galilee, and manifested forth his glory; and his disciples believed on him (John 2:11).

The text when put back into its context becomes the study passage.

Context – The outline from a Study Bible Edition of the *Authorized King James Version*, shows *the* study passage as (John 2:1-12). When studying a narrative with a special feature you may need both the Narrative and Miracle Exegesis. If the narrative is about the miracle, then the Miracle Exegesis is the tool of choice.

Literary Form – The literary form is a Narrative with a miracle special feature. Please refer to Appendix II Literary Forms Quick Chart p., 129.

Miracle Exegesis

Contextual Rules - Four rules governs valid reasons for going outside the study passage. (For discussion on valid rules, refer to pp., 25 and 26). No rules are applicable for this study passage. **Background** – The background found in (John 2:1-12) gives us the stage or setting in which the event took place. In this case, it is the same as the context. Jesus attends the marriage feast in Cana of Galilee performs a miracle by (changes water to wine). This is the first sign of His messianic ministry, as recorded by John. Check the outline in a Study Bible Edition of the *Authorized King James Version*. **Panoramic View** – The panoramic view is the (Book of John, I, II, and III Epistle of John and the Book of Revelations). The panoramic view verifies the author, collection of literature, theological themes, custom and traditions of the Holy lands, first response of the hearers and relevant topography. Laney Carl J, *Concise Bible Atlas: A Geographical Survey of Bible History* records that Jesus gave his disciples a foretaste of kingdom blessings by turning spring water into wedding wine (John 2:1-11; cf. Joel 3:18). [1]

SECTION THREE – Contextual Inquiry

Who is the main speaker, teacher, preacher writer or other? Jesus of Nazareth is the speaker (John 2:7). Who is speaking-helps us to determine whether the passage content is the words of Jesus, God, Satan, demons, angels or man. *Search Rule:* First look in the text, context and background - validation should come in or before the text. *Jesus saith unto them, Fill the waterpots with water. And they filled them up to the brim* (John 2:7).

Miracle Exegesis

What is the authority: claims, divine call, commission or other? Jesus of Nazareth claims to be the "Son of Man." This claim reveals his earthly title. Please refer to Chart 4-4 page 33. *And he saith unto him, Verily, verily, I say unto you, Hereafter ye shall see heaven open, and the angels of God ascending and descending upon the Son of man* (John 1:51). Idioma is the particular usage of words and phrases, for example, "Son of Man" is an idioma. [2]

Bullinger *(figura)* under Synecdoche considers the ordinary meaning of *"Son of Man"*; but the definite article, the phrase have a special idiomatic usage of its own. No one was ever so called but Christ Himself. He first thus calls Himself in John 1:51 (52). The reference is to the first occurrence of the phrase in Psalms viii, where the title involves universal dominion in the earth. Adam, the first man, lost dominion. Restoration takes place in "the Son of man," the second man," "the Lord from Heaven." [3] [Please refer to notes on p., 93 for an alternative view.]

Who is the audience of the speaker, teacher, preacher, writer or other? The audience included the multitude, Jesus' mother, and servants, governor of the house, bridegroom, Jesus' brethren (siblings) and disciples (John 2:4-5; 9; 12).

Miracle Exegesis

> SECTION FOUR – Applying the Exegetical Methods

- Discovering the Central Truth

The Miracle Exegesis is the tool of choice. Please refer to Miracle Exegesis Appendix III, p., 135.

Book of John, Chapter 2

2:1
And the third day there was a marriage in Cana of Galilee; and the mother of Jesus was there:

2:2
And both Jesus was called, and his disciples, to the marriage.

2:3
And when they wanted wine, the mother of Jesus saith unto him, They have no wine.

2:4
Jesus saith unto her, Woman, what have I to do with thee? mine hour is not yet come. Idioma (See John 1:51, page 88.) [4]

2:5
His mother saith unto the servants, Whatsoever he saith unto you, do it.

2:6
And there were set there six water pots of stone, after the manner of the purifying of the Jews, containing two or three firkins apiece.

Miracle Exegesis

2:7

Jesus saith unto them, Fill the water pots with water. And they filled them up to the brim. Genitive of Origin and Efficient Cause (Genitive of the Contents) means denoting that with which anything is filled. 5

2:8

And he saith unto them, Draw out now, and bear unto the governor of the feast. And they bare it.

2:9

When the ruler of the feast had tasted the water that was made wine, and knew not whence it was: (but the servants which drew the water knew;) the governor of the feast called the bridegroom, Epitrechon is a parenthetic addition by way of statement thrown in, not complete in itself, for example *(but the servants which drew the water knew)* 6

2:10

And saith unto him, Every man at the beginning doth set forth good wine; and when men have well drunk, then that which is worse: but thou hast kept the good wine until now.

2:11

This beginning of miracles did Jesus in Cana of Galilee, and manifested forth his glory; and his disciples believed on him.

2:12

After this he went down to Capernaum, he, and his mother, and his brethren, and his disciples: and they continued there not many days.

Miracle Exegesis

- Miracle Exegesis

Exegetical Notes: It is necessary to vary the components of the Miracle Exegesis to fit this occasion since the miracle is not deliverance.

Dialogue

- **Request** - Mary (the mother of Jesus): "No more wine, Verse 3"
- **Response** - (1) Jesus said: "Mine hour is not yet come (John 2:4b)" (2) Jesus command servants: "Fill water pots with water (John 2:7) "
- **Results** - "Water changed to wine (John 2:9)"
- **Response To Miracle** – "His disciple believed on him (John 2:11c)"

What is the Central Truth? The Central Truth is not just verse 11 but John 2:11b, c. The miracle by definition serves as a compass pointing to a saying. In this narrative, the Apostle John (an observer) gives the saying to us. With this saying, he gives us both the purpose of and the response to the miracle at Cana. With this in mind, does the number of water pots, alcohol content or the superior quality of the wine have any significance? Does it matter that Jesus choice of drink (wine) as was the custom was served at a wedding feast? These questions when compared to the saying given by the Apostle and the response of the Disciples seem trivial. Please keep in mind the drink of choice, in this culture was wine rather than water.

Miracle Exegesis

SECTION FIVE – Exegetical Inquiry

How should we accept this Scripture? John records *"This beginning of miracles did Jesus in Cana of Galilee, and manifested forth his glory; and his disciples believed on him, v. 11).* Its meaning is exclusive yet clear. All present-day Bible readers should accept it as *literal*. How do we decide its application? Discover the application by examining as clear as possible the intent of the narrative. God manifested His glory in Israel's history and continues to manifest Himself in the church today. Therefore, when the teaching transcends dispensational theology, it is clearly a Biblical *principle*. How do we decide its profitability? Choose from doctrine, reproof, correction and instruction in righteousness. This is clearly *doctrine* since the manifested glory of God in Christ is the purpose for this miracle.

Miracle Exegesis

Notes

1. Laney Carl J, *Concise Bible Atlas: A Geographical Survey of Bible History*, Hendrickson Publishers, 1998, p. 202.

2. Bullinger E. W., *Figures of Speech Used in the Bible*, Baker Book House, Grand Rapids, Michigan, 1968, pp. 819, 842.

3. *Ibid.*, p. 842.
I challenge Bullinger's notion the title *"Son of Man"* involves universal dominion (Psalms 8). The title is also used by God to refer to Ezekiel, a priest. Christ, also a priest used the title to refer to himself as understood by Bullinger. The title, however, has more to do with the purpose of God for redemption, rather than universal dominion. *The word of the Lord came expressly unto Ezekiel the priest, the son of Buzi in the land of the Chaldeans by the river Chebar, and the hand of the lord was there upon him. (Ezekiel 1:3). And he said unto me, Son of man, stand upon thy feet, and I will speak unto thee* (Ezekiel 2:1). Please refer to the Chart 4-4 Hierarchy Authority Claims of Jesus of Nazareth, page 33.

4. *Ibid.*, p. 842.

5. *Ibid.*, p. 1001.

6. *Ibid.*, pp. 472, 473.

Chapter 11

Prophecy Exegesis

Text – Matthew 25:34

SECTION ONE – Study Method

The Dialectical Method of Biblical Exegesis is a Revelation Paradigm for Students Taught by the Holy Spirit Studying Scripture.

SECTION TWO – Determining – Textual – Historical – Literary Context

Text - *Then shall the King say unto them on his right hand, Come, ye blessed of my Father, inherit the kingdom prepared for you from the foundation of the world* **(Matthew 25:34).** The text when put back into its context becomes the study passage.

Context - Using the outline taken from an *Authorized King James* Version Study Bible, the study passage is (Matthew 25:31-46). Studying prophetic narratives requires an examination of the sovereignty of God. God's sovereignty to appoint representatives who declare His messages through warnings and promises denotes sovereignty. They revealed the sinful practices of the people, warned about judgment to come, and called the people to repentance. The divine appointed individuals received God's message through dreams, visions, angels, and direct encounters with the Lord, also related these messages in oral, visual, and written form.

Prophecy Exegesis

Literary Form – The literary form is a Prophetic Narrative. The narrative is prophetic because it contains promises of end time events about judging the Gentiles occurring in a future timeline set by God. Please refer to Appendix II Literary Forms Quick Chart p., 129.

Contextual Rules - Four rules govern valid reasons for going outside the study passage. (For discussion on valid rules, refer to pp., 25 and 26). In this study, rule number two considers the passage composition that uses prophetic literature.

Rule number two is unfulfilled prophesy (Matthew 25:31) about events that happen at the Second Coming of Christ. Jesus predicts judging the Gentiles at the throne of his glory (Matthew 25:31). This event takes place in the future as recorded in (Revelation 19:11). This Judgment of Gentiles is one of five judgments recorded in Scripture. Also see the judgments of believers sins (John 5:24); self (1 Corinthians 11:31-32); works (II Corinthians 5:10) and the wicked dead (Revelation 20:11-15).

Background – The background found in (Matthew 24:1 - 25:46) gives us the stage or setting in which the event took place. Look for such events as the changing from one location to another, or giving a revelation to more than one group or changing subject matter. Check the outline in a Study Bible Edition of the *Authorized King James Version*. Matthew records Jesus predictions of judgment at His Second Coming. The parable of the ten virgins and talents leads up to our study passage and serves as the background for the text.

Prophecy Exegesis

Panoramic View – The panoramic view is the Book of Matthew the Apostle whose author's name is listed in (10:1-4). The panoramic view verifies the author, collection of literature, theological themes, custom and traditions of the Holy lands, first response of the hearers and relevant topography.

Where is the Mount Olives according to Laney? Just east of Jerusalem and across the Kidron Valley is the Mount of Olives (2,700 feet). The "mount" is a north-south ridge that parallels the valley. Jesus visited the mount (John 8:1; Mark 11:1; Matthew 24:3; 26:30), prayed in the Garden of Gethsemane at its foot (Matthew 26:30), and went up from its summit into heaven (Acts 1:9-12). [1]

SECTION THREE – Contextual Inquiry

Jesus of Nazareth is the teacher (Matthew 24:4). "He sat upon the Mount of Olives (verse 3) accommodating the privacy sought by the disciples. *Search Rule:* First look in the text, context and background - validation should come in or before the text.

And as he sat upon the mount of Olives, the disciples came unto him privately, saying, Tell us, when shall these things be? and what shall be the sign of thy coming, and of the end of the world?

And Jesus answered and said unto them, Take heed that no man deceive you (Matthew 24:3, 4).

Prophecy Exegesis

What is the authority: claims, divine call, commission or other? Jesus claimed to be the *"Son of Man"* as recorded in (Matthew 25:31). The phrase "Son of Man" is a Idioma. [2] Also see previous discussion about this figure of speech, John 1:51 p. 88 and John 2:4 p. 89.

When the Son of man shall come in his glory, and all the holy angels with him, then shall he sit upon the throne of his glory (Matthew 25:31).

Who is the audience of the speaker, teacher, preacher, writer or other? Jesus disciples received this teaching in private as recorded by (Matthew 24:3).

And as he sat upon the mount of Olives, the disciples came unto him privately, saying, Tell us, when shall these things be? and what shall be the sign of thy coming, and of the end of the world? (Matthew 24:3).

Prophecy Exegesis

SECTION FOUR – Applying the Exegetical Methods

- Discovering the Central Truth

The Prophetic Exegesis is the tool of choice. It works best with narratives even when they contain special features, such as prophecy. Some narratives may require combining of exegetical methods because of complexity. Please refer to Narrative Exegesis Appendix III, p. 132.

Book of Matthew, Chapter 25

25:31
When the Son of man shall come in his glory, and all the holy angels with him, then shall he sit upon the throne of his glory: Idioma – (See John 1:51 p., 88.

25:32
And before him shall be gathered all nations: and he shall separate them one from another, as a shepherd divideth his sheep from the goats:

25:33
And he shall set the sheep on his right hand, but the goats on the left.

25:34
Then shall the King say unto them on his right hand, Come, ye blessed of my Father, inherit the kingdom prepared for you from the foundation of the world:

25:35
For I was an hungred, and ye gave me meat: I was thirsty, and ye gave me drink: I was a stranger, and ye took me in:

25:36

Naked, and ye clothed me: I was sick, and ye visited me: I was in prison, and ye came unto me. Synecdoche (Of The Whole) indicates the whole is put for one of its parts. In this case, "naked" is put for being scantily clothed, or poorly clad. Also, see verse 43. 3

[ ]

25:37

Then shall the righteous answer him, saying, Lord, when saw we thee an hungred, and fed thee? or thirsty, and gave thee drink?

25:38

When saw we thee a stranger, and took thee in? or naked, and clothed thee?

25:39

Or when saw we thee sick, or in prison, and came unto thee? Dialogismos is used when we represent one or more persons as speaking about a thing, instead of saying it ourselves: Dialogue, verses 37-39. 4

[ ]

25:40

And the King shall answer and say unto them, Verily I say unto you, Inasmuch as ye have done it unto one of the least of these my brethren, ye have done it unto me.

25:41

Then shall he say also unto them on the left hand, Depart from me, ye cursed, into everlasting fire, prepared for the devil and his angels:

Prophecy Exegesis

25:42

For I was an hungred, and ye gave me no meat: I was thirsty, and ye gave me no drink:

25:43

I was a stranger, and ye took me not in: naked, and ye clothed me not: sick, and in prison, and ye visited me not.

25:44

Then shall they also answer him, saying, Lord, when saw we thee an hungred, or athirst, or a stranger, or naked, or sick, or in prison, and did not minister unto thee?

25:45

Then shall he answer them, saying, Verily I say unto you, Inasmuch as ye did it not to one of the least of these, ye did it not to me.

25:46

And these shall go away into everlasting punishment: but the righteous into life eternal.

Prophecy Exegesis

- Applying the Prophecy Exegesis

  This prophecy exegesis works with the List Exegesis, when examining figures of speech.

There are three steps in studying prophetic narratives. First, determine the Scriptural context of prophecy. Second, discover if the prophecy fulfillment is future or past. Third, discover the time line of Bible Prophecy when applicable. For a discussion on the Prophecy Exegesis, see Appendix III, page 136.

- Prophecy Exegesis

JUDGEMENT OF THE NATIONS

SHEEP	GOATS
<ul><li>Matthew 25:35-36</li><li>Regarding Jesus Brethren - Israel</li><li>Judgment Kingdom of Heaven v.34</li></ul>	<ul><li>Matthew 25:42-45</li><li>Regarding Jesus Brethren - Israel</li><li>Judgment Lake of Fire v.41</li></ul>

The time line of Bible prophecy about Judging Nations recorded in Matthew 25:31-46 has future fulfillment at the "Second Coming".

What is the Central Truth? Jesus summarized Judging Nations. *"And these shall go away into everlasting punishment: but the righteous into life eternal* (Matthew 25:46).

SECTION FIVE – Exegetical Inquiry

How should we accept this Scripture? The Lord's answer is *literal*. The signs are recognizable for those living at that time. How do we decide its application? Discover the application by examining as clear as possible the intent of Jesus prediction. Jesus prediction points to God's purpose for the end time destiny of the civilization regarding His brethren, Israel. When this is the case, it is a prediction about the *world*. How do we decide its profitability? Choose from doctrine, reproof, correction and instruction in righteousness. This prediction establishes *doctrine* about the sovereignty of God and the reliability of His covenant with Israel.

Notes

1. Laney J Carl, *Concise Bible Atlas: A Geographical Survey of Bible History*, Hendrickson Publishers, 1999, p. 173.

2. Bullinger E. W., *Figures of Speech Used in the Bible*, Baker Book House, Grand Rapids, Michigan, 1968, pp. 819, 842.

3. *Ibid.*, p. 637.

4. *Ibid.*, p. 956.

📖 Chapter 12

Prayer Exegesis

Text - Ephesians 1:22-23

SECTION ONE – *Study Method*

The Dialectical Method of Biblical Exegesis is a Revelation Paradigm for Students Taught by the Holy Spirit Studying Scripture.

SECTION TWO – Determining – Textual – Historical – Literary Context

Text - Ephesians 1:22-23

And hath put all things under his feet, and gave him to be the head over all things to the church,
Which is his body, the fulness of him that filleth all in all.
(Ephesians 1:22, 23). The text when put back into its context becomes the study passage.

Context – Using the outline taken from a Study Bible Edition of the *Authorized King James Version*, the study passage is (Ephesians 1: 15-23). When studying prayer keep in mind that God's Spirit commune with us through Scripture, dreams, visions, songs, the universe, life's blessings, curses and so forth. We communicate with God through the Holy Spirit. The Spirit of God abode with us in worship, praise, dance, so forth, as well as prayer. Both communion and communication must take place within fellowship with God. The prerequisite for this fellowship is the New Birth.

Prayer Exegesis

Literary Form – The literary form is an Epistle, which contains a prayer. Please refer to Appendix II Literary Forms Quick Chart p., 129.

Contextual Rules - Four rules govern valid reasons for going outside the study passage. (For discussion on valid rules, refer to pp., 25 and 26). Let us examine two verses in the study passage, one under rule one and the other under rule two. No other rules apply for this study passage. The (R superscription) above the passage marks a valid reference under rule one.

[R] *That the God of our Lord Jesus Christ, the Father of glory, may give unto you the spirit of wisdom and revelation in the knowledge of him* (Ephesians 1:17).

- RULE NO 1

Ephesians 1:17 is a Christian application of the Kingdom Principle of John 20:17

And [R] hath put all things under his feet, and gave him to be the head over all things to the church (Ephesians 1:22).

- RULE NO 2

Ephesians 1:22a is prophecy (Daniel 7:13, 14) fulfilled in Jesus of Nazareth. Ephesians 1:22b is a Christian application of the fulfilled prophecy concerning Jesus as head of the New Testament Church (Matthew 28:18).

Prayer Exegesis

Background – The background found in (Ephesians 1: 15-23) usually gives us the stage or setting in which the event took place. Studying an epistle, however, we look for themes and grouping of issues. The church at Ephesus is rich beyond measure in Jesus Christ, yet living as beggars, and only because they are ignorant of their wealth, they relegate themselves to living as spiritual paupers. Paul begins in chapters 1 – 3 outlining the content of their Christian faith. The epistles are topical and grouped around common themes. Check the outline in a Study Bible Edition of the *Authorized King James Version*.
Panoramic View – The panoramic view is the (Book of Ephesians). The panoramic view verifies the author, collection of literature, theological themes, custom and traditions of the Holy lands, first response of the hearers and relevant topography.

SECTION THREE – Contextual Inquiry

Who is the main speaker, teacher, preacher writer or other? Paul is the writer as recorded in Ephesians 1:1. *Search Rule:* First look in the text, context and background - validation should come in or before the text. *Paul, an apostle of Jesus Christ by the will of God, to the saints, which are at Ephesus, and to the faithful in Christ Jesus* (Ephesians 1:1). What is the authority: claims, divine call, commission or other? Paul is an Apostle. Please refer to Chart 7-7 p., 48. Who is the audience of the speaker, teacher, preacher, writer or other? Paul writes to the saints, which are at Ephesus, and to the faithful in Christ Jesus. The term saint means sanctifies or set apart. Paul is writing to the "born-again, baptized believers in Christ Jesus, who live in Ephesus (Ephesians 1:1).

Prayer Exegesis

> # SECTION FOUR – Applying the Exegetical Methods

- Discovering the Central Truth

The Prayer Exegesis is the tool of choice. Please refer to Prayer Exegesis Appendix III, p., 139.

Ephesians 1: 15-23

1:15

Wherefore I also, after I heard of your faith in the Lord Jesus, and love unto all the saints,

1:16

Cease not to give thanks for you, making mention of you in my prayers;

1:17

That the God of our Lord Jesus Christ, the Father of glory, may give unto you the spirit of wisdom and revelation in the knowledge of him:

1:18

The eyes of your understanding being enlightened; that ye may know what is the hope of his calling, and what the riches of the glory of his inheritance in the saints Antiptosis as a figure of exchanging of one case for another. [1] Genitive of Partition, Separation, or Ablation is a figure that closely connected with the fundamental idea of the genitive, which answers the question, Whence? [2]

Prayer Exegesis

1:19

And what is the exceeding greatness of his power to us-ward who believe, according to the working of his mighty power,

1:20

Which he wrought in Christ, when he raised him from the dead, and set him at his own right hand in the heavenly places,

1:21

Far above all principality, and power, and might, and dominion, and every name that is named, not only in this world, but also in that which is to come:

1:22

And hath put all things under his feet, and gave him to be the head over all things to the church,

1:23

Which is his body, the fulness of him that filleth all in all. Parembole is an insertion besides, between, or answer others; and the name is used when the sentence interposed is independent and complete in itself; and would make complete sense if it were separated from the sentence, which it divides, for example Ephesians 1: 19-23. [3]

Prayer Exegesis

- Prayer Exegesis

The act of praying denotes a relationship wherein prayer is an act of worship.

Prophetic Prayer has four components:

1. Communion – Listen to God speaks, for example Scriptures, preaching, bible study.
2. Communication – Talk, petition, give thanks, etc.
3. Fellowship with God - Communion and Communication only operates within the context of this fellowship, in Faith expecting results.
4. Exegetical Considerations
    a. Does the Prayer have the right standing (justification) and status (sanctification) with which one prays? [X] Yes (Ephesians 1:17a)   [ ] No
    b. Does the Text contain evidence of communion with God? [ ] Yes   [X] No
    c. Does the Text indicate an answer to the Prayer or (Prophetic Prayer)? [ ] Yes   [ ] No   [X] Unknown
    d. Identify the elements of the prayer

Relationship: Ephesians 1:17a- Paul indicates both his and the saints relationship with the "God of our Lord Jesus Christ the Father of glory."

Petition/Thanksgiving, Repentance, for example, Ephesians 1:17a- Paul petition God to give the saints the *"spirit of wisdom and revelation in the knowledge of him."* Wisdom is knowledge guided by understanding.

Prayer Exegesis

Revelation is an uncovering of something previous hidden. This short listing is hierarchal. In Ephesians 1:18-23 Paul outlined specific knowledge of him (Christ Jesus) wherein the saints would benefit from the spirit of wisdom and revelation. (Also, see Proverbs 4:7).

Prayer Answer: Unknown - Generally one may conclude that since Paul only wrote one epistle to Ephesus, perhaps the saints received the spirit of wisdom & revelation.

What is the Central Truth? (Ephesians 1:17) That *the God of our Lord Jesus Christ, the Father of glory, may give unto you the spirit of wisdom and revelation in the knowledge of him* (Ephesians 1:17).

> **SECTION FIVE – Exegetical Inquiry**

How should we accept this Scripture? Paul's prayer and its meaning is exclusive yet clear. All present-day Bible readers should accept it as *literal*. How do we decide its application? Discover the application by examining as clear as possible the intent of the letter. Paul prays to the God of our Lord Jesus Christ within a fellowship relationship expecting results. This plea for revelation is clearly for the *New Testament Church* and profitable for *doctrine*.

Notes

1. Bullinger E. W., *Figures of Speech Used in the Bible*, Baker Book House, Grand Rapids, Michigan, 1968, .p. 508.

2. *Ibid.*, pp. 1001 – 1002.

3. *Ibid.*, pp. 476, 477.

📖 Chapter 13

The Dialogue extended by using Web Forums for discussion.

Section six – This section is only accessible on the Worldwide Web. The Bible declares that *"Knowing this first, which no prophecy of the scripture is of any private interpretation."* Therefore, these supervised forums designed to encourage a study of the Bible invites apologist from the community of faith to take part in and add to the effectiveness of the Dialectical Method. Using web forums to complement the book requires publishers' web conferencing software and reader access to the worldwide web. Let us examine one of the most common features on a website: a discussion forum, one of the primary tools for building online communities and making discussion are available on the Internet. The created discussion forum fulfills the following requirements: have a list of categories, have forums grouped in categories and moderated by a discussion leader. In addition, users must register in the system to be able to post to the forums. Reading messages, however, requires no registration. Site management governed within the site by checking for administrator privileges on login and displaying the proper administrative tools. Qualified moderators selected for web discussion forums may come from several different Christian traditions. Preserving a high degree of objectivity in matters of scholarship and verifiable historical fact using research methods is of the highest priority. The Dialectical Method does not need ecumenical cooperation, theological debates or traditional denominational views of former years.

Web Forums

It needs a dependence on the Holy Spirit for illumination. For theological inquiry of this importance, administrators, faculty, alumni and enrolled students of Smith Chapel Bible College may not serve as moderators. The precondition for selecting conference forum moderators is the successful completion and certification of a (twelve-week) Dialectical Method moderator's course rather than pedigree or credentials from Ivy League post-secondary institutions.

Summary of Key Features
This section is for the user.
- Intuitive user interface that works with any browser
- User interface fully customizable with downloadable "skins"
- Formatting, HTML validation, and in-line image upload
- Search capability (by date or keyword)
- E-mail notice of new posts in "subscribed" areas
- User interface available in English and 14 other languages

This section is for the moderators and administrator.
- Comprehensive browser-based administration tool set
- Unlimited thread depth, allowing organization of material within topics
- Configure public or private posting for each discussion topic
- User account management tools

Web Forums

Besides the myriad of other potential uses, the design of web conferencing software makes it well suited for use in education. Administrators, faculty, alumni and students may take part in discussions to strengthen educational promise of the Dialectical Method.

Smith Chapel Bible College Web site designed for academic use, offering an intuitive user link and powerful URL is www.scbc.edu. The web conferencing forum initially divided into four forums with assigned moderators.

I. The Pentateuch Forum – This online conference begins with a general introduction to the Pentateuch as a whole. Next, the moderator discovers the main events of each of the five books and prepares study sheets.

II. The Historical Books Forum – This online conference begins with the twelve books of the Bible from Joshua through Esther, and prepares study sheets on each book.

III. The Four-Gospel Forum – This online conference begins with the chronological harmony of the life of Christ in the four Gospel. Each Gospel is studied individually with distinctive contributions recognized from the perspective of the gospel writer.

Web Forums

IV. Eschatology Forum - The online conference begins with the systematic presentation of the Bible's account of the future. Topics covered include: approaches to the study, rapture, second coming, intermediate state, tribulation, resurrection, judgments, millennium, and the eternal state.

Conclusion

Section One: The study method begins with a prayerful affirmation that the Holy Spirit engages us in the study of the Holy Bible. Seeking wisdom and receiving revelation is a paradigm for Students Taught by the Holy Spirit Studying Scripture. The four foundational passages for the Dialectical Method defines the student as chosen, the Holy Spirit as teacher, the study method as approved unto God and the study passages as inspired by God. This affirmation positions us for textual revelation in section two.

Section Two: Determining the textual, historical and literary context begins with the text, also known as, the study passage. Since the text is always out of context, the first task is to put the text back into its proper context by discovering its literary form. The contextual rules control four valid reasons for going outside the context. This systematic approach ensures a continuity of biblical revelation rather than a topical or word study of Scripture. The text once placed in its context fits nicely into its background. The stage or setting consideration may be narrow or broad as discovered by the student. The Dialectical Method allows for background flexibility. With the background firmly fixed, the big picture of the panoramic view is clear. The validation of the author when historical possible, collection of literature, theological themes, custom and traditions of the Holy lands and relevant topography are essential for rightly dividing the word of truth. With the passage open for inspection in section two, the student is ready for further contextual inquiry in section three.

Conclusion

Section Three: Contextual Inquiry begins with discovery of the role of the main character, whether speaking, teaching, preaching or writing. This requires a search of the text, context and background for both words or deeds of the main character, and discovery comes before the text. Next, the discovery of the main character's claims, divine call and commission authenticates the issues of authority. This section would not be complete without the identification of the audience and the connection between the main characters. In the Pentateuch, for example, this connection may be the Abrahamic Covenant, in the historical books it may be the "Spirit of the Lord is upon them." In the four gospels, it may be the circle of influence of Jesus of Nazareth. In the Acts of the Apostles, it may be the Holy Spirit. In the New Testament church, it may be the apostolic authority. After extracting and preparing what seems to be an unfolding drama, you are now ready to make application with one of the seven exegetical methods in section four.

Section Four: Applying exegetical methods begin with matching the literary form with its exegetical counterpart. The simplest is the list exegesis used to discover word definition and *(figura)* of each passage. It also works well with other exegesis. The decode exegesis, for example, works excellent with wisdom literature and usually requires the list exegesis to deal with the various literary devices. The narrative, epistle, miracle, prophecy and prayer exegesis works with each specific literary form. The study passage when illuminated has its original meaning made clear. This clears the way for discovering the study passage application in section five.

Conclusion

Section Five: Exegetical inquiry begins with receiving the revelation as literal or figuratively. Once the literal understanding is obvious, the study passage (present-day) application for the Church, World or Israel becomes self-evident. Finally, the study passage profitability is important to ensure it present-day application.

Students using the Dialectical Method are dependent on the Spirit of the Lord for Scriptural illumination.

AMEN

Bibliography

Bibliography

- Bible

Holy Bible, The New Open Bible, Study Edition, Thomas Nelson Publishers, 1990.

Watchman Bible Software, Bible software for Windows 95, 98, 2000, NT, ME and XP, McElroy Publishing, 2003.

- Books

Bullinger E. W., *Figures of Speech Used in the Bible,* Baker Book House, Grand Rapids, Michigan, Twenty-third printing, March 2003.

Danker, Frederick W. *Multipurpose Tools for Bible Study.* 4th edition. Minneapolis: Fortress, 1993.

Fee, Gordon D. *New Testament Exegesis: A Handbook for Students and Pastors.* Philadelphia: Westminister, 1983.

Harrington, Daniel J. *Interpreting the New Testament: A Practical Guide.* Wilmington: Michael Glazier, 1979.

Hayes, John H. and Carl R. Holladay. *Biblical Exegesis: A Beginner's Handbook.* Atlanta: John Knox, 1982.

Hegel, G. W. F., *The Philosophical System.* Contributors: Howard P. Kainz – author, Ohio University Press. Athens, 1998.

Bibliography

Holdcroft Thomas L., *The Four Gospels*, Third Edition, CeeTeeC Publishing, 1999.

Laney Carl J, Concise Bible Atlas: *A Geographical Survey of Bible History*, Hendrickson Publishers, 1998.

Long Thomas G, *Preaching and the Literary Forms of the Bible*, Fortress Press, 1990.

Mears, Henrietta C. *What the Bible is All About*, Regal Books, 1997.

Richardson Alan, editor, A *Dictionary of Christian Theology*, The Westminster Press, Philadelphia, 1967.

Soulen, Richard N. *Handbook of Biblical Criticism*. 2nd edition. Atlanta: John Knox, 1981.

Stewart, Douglas. *Old Testament Exegesis: A Primer for Students and Pastors*. Second edition. Philadelphia: Westminster, 1984.

Wald, Oletta. *The Joy of Discovery in Bible Study*. Minneapolis: Fortress, 1975.

- Dictionary

A Dictionary of Christian Theology, Edited by Alan Richardson, The Westminster Press, Philadelphia, 1969.

Butler Trent C, Ph.D., General Editor, *Holman Bible Dictionary*, Exhaustive Theological, Scriptural Pronouncing Guide, Holman Bible Publishers, Nashville, Tennessee, 1991.

Appendix I

Appendix

I. Dialectical Study Sheet

Dialectical Method of Biblical Exegesis

SECTION ONE - STUDY METHOD

Goal: Do you seek Revelation rather than just Bible knowledge? Do you receive that: "Wisdom is the principle thing; therefore get wisdom: and with all thy getting get understanding (KJV, Proverbs. 4:7"). If so, please check the following objectives:

Objectives:

[ ] You learn to engage Holy Scripture (*Authorized King James Version*), while prayerfully depending on the Holy Spirit for illumination, rather than the professor.

[ ] You learn the Biblical relationship between "Study and Rightly Dividing" the Word of Truth (2 Tim 2:15-16). This method is the:

"Dialectical Method of Biblical Exegesis"

1. **Students:**	2. **Holy Spirit:**	3. **Study:**	4. **Scripture:**
"Ye have not chosen me, but I have chosen you, and ordained you that ye should go and bring forth fruit ... (John 15:16)" **taught by the ...**	"But the Comforter, which is the Holy Ghost, whom the Father will send in my name, he shall teach you all things ...,(John 14:26)"	"Study to show thyself approved unto God ... (2 Timothy 2:15-16)"	"All Scripture is given by inspiration of God ... (2 Timothy 3:16-17)"

121

Appendix I

SECTION TWO - DETERMINING ~ TEXTUAL * HISTORICAL * LITERARY * CONTEXT

> **Text:** _____
> **Lesson No.** _____
> The text is always the Scripture verses read - beginning of Scripture that starts the study.
> **Context** _____
>
> **Literary Form:** _____

The <u>context</u> is synonymous with the literary form, often referred to as the form of composition. Understanding <u>literary</u> forms helps us to read, interpret, and make application of biblical truths. Without a working knowledge of biblical literature, we will not be able divide the word of truth rightly according to 2 Timothy 2:15-16. **Reference:** Long Thomas G, *Preaching and the Literary Forms of the Bible*, Fortress Press, 1990.

Contextual Rules: There are four valid reasons for going outside the context. **Reference** Holdcroft Thomas L, *The Four Gospels,* Third Edition, CeeTeeC Publishing, 1999.

> 1. When the study passage quotes a Scripture or gives the revelation truth of a passage.
> 2. Prophetic literature whether fulfilled or not. Fulfilled prophecy requires that you include the reference to its fulfillment while unfulfilled prophecy requires a "Time Line of Bible Prophecy".
> 3. When answering questions in Section Three - contextual inquiry.
> 4. When the study passage has parallel or synoptic events recorded in Scripture.

Appendix I

Label and show your reasons below:

_____
_____
_____
_____
_____
_____
_____
_____
_____
_____
_____
_____
_____
_____
_____
_____
_____
_____

Background: _____

The background gives us the stage or setting in which the event took place. Look for such events as the changing from one location to another, or giving a revelation to more than one group. **Reference:** Check the outline in the *Authorized King James Version*.

Panoramic View: _____

The panoramic view confirms the author, collection of literature, theological themes, custom and traditions of the Holy lands, first response of the hearers and relevant topography. **Reference:** Laney Carl J, *Concise Bible Atlas: A Geographical Survey of Bible History*, Hendrickson Publishers, 1998.

Appendix I

SECTION THREE- CONTEXTUAL INQUIRY
1. ASK WHO IS THE MAIN: [ ] SPEAKER [ ] TEACHER [ ] PREACHER [ ] WRITER [ ] (OTHER) _____

Name: _____
Scripture Reference: Saying: _____
                          Deeds: _____

Who speaks or reference to the main character in the passage helps us to discover whether the passage content is the words or deeds of God, Satan, demons, angels or man. Search **Rule:** First look in the text, context and background for either the words or deeds - validation should come in or before the text. When Scripture validation is outside the background, you need two references. A Proper name, for example "Jesus of Nazareth said..." and a Pronoun for example, "He said."

_____
_____
_____
_____

Appendix I

2.   ASK BY WHAT AUTHORITY? [ ] CLAIMS? [ ] DIVINE CALL?
[ ] COMMISSION? [ ] (OTHER) _____

Name: _____
List Authority (s): _____
Scripture Reference: _____

We should become familiar with customs and traditions of the Holy Land. The customs and traditions provide the background for God's revelation, also known as, the "Central Truth." The words of a Prophet, for example, might carry more authority than that of a King or perhaps even a Priest depending on the context. Jesus of Nazareth validates only His claims as Emanuel. All other who are His disciples, including you and I make a scriptural validation of our CLAIM, CALL and COMMISSION.

Hierarchy authority claims of Jesus of Nazareth.

(1) Jesus of Nazareth Asserts that He is God for example, Luke 4:8; 12
(2) "I AM" Saying for example, John 15:1
(3) TITLES 3.1 Son of God = Divine title 3.2 Son of David = Jewish title 3.3 Son of man = Earthly title
(4) DIVINE ATTRIBUTES: 4.1 Omnipotent 4.2 Omniscience 4.3 Omnipresence

Appendix I

3. ASK TO WHOM: [ ] SPOKEN [ ] TAUGHT [ ]
PREACHED [ ] WRITTEN
   [ ] (OTHER) _____

Name: _____
Scripture Reference: _____

CIRCLES OF INFLUENCE

1. Jesus and John
2. Peter, James and John (Inner Circle)
3. The Twelve Apostles
4. Jesus Friends, the Disciples 120, 70, 400
5. The Multitude - Jews, Scribes, Publicans,
6. Not Applicable

Select the Circle of Influence:_____

Appendix I

SECTION FOUR – APPLYING EXEGETICAL METHODS
[ ] List Exegesis [ ] Decode Exegesis [ ] Narrative Exegesis [ ] Epistles Exegesis [ ] Miracle Exegesis [ ] Prophecy Exegesis [ ] Prayer Exegesis

What is the Central Truth? The simple approach to understanding Scripture is revealing and yet problematic. It is best not to read into a passage one's imagination rather rely on the Holy Spirit for its literal teachings. The Central Truth illumination comes from the Holy Spirit (John 14:26). Section four has two components:

A. *Discovery* – Identify the figure of speech used in the passage, Ref. Bullinger, 2003.
_____
_____
_____
_____
_____

B. *Exegesis* - Select one or more of the seven exegeses appropriate for this study.
_____
_____
_____
_____
_____

THE CENTRAL TRUTH _____

Appendix I

SECTION FIVE - EXEGETICAL INQUIRY
1. How should we accept this Scripture?
   [ ] Literal or [ ] Figuratively
2. How do we determine its application? God's Plan and Purpose about the Church, the World and Israel, spoken by the Major and Minor Prophets, consist of one fourth of all Scripture. Therefore, Scripture application both understood and literally fulfilled reveals application for one of the following:

[ ] CHURCH is a biblical definition of church must be about the relationship of the believer with Christ Jesus rather than a building (Matthew 16:18).

[ ] WORLD means the god of this world is Satan. (1 John 4:4; 2 Corinthians 4:4)

[ ] ISRAEL refers to descendants of Jacob beginning as a nation in Egypt (Genesis 49:16, 28; Exodus 1:12, 20).

[ ] BIBLICAL PRINCIPLE is a truth that transcends dispensational theology regarding the Old Testament and the New Testament. For example Acts 10:43.

   3. How do we determine its profitability?

[ ] Doctrine is a teaching that is either truth or error. Revelation truth is of God while error or lies are of Satan.
[ ] Reproof is a cutting rebuke for misconduct
[ ] Correction means punishment designed to restore
[ ] Instruction in righteousness means how must we live uprightness before God as shown through Faith & Practice.

Appendix II

II. Literary Forms Quick Chart

NOTES ON DETERMINING LITERARY FORMS

Proverb	Theme	Wisdom	Poetic	Revealing Insight	Moral Point
Parable	Theme	Story	Simile	Common Experience	Moral Point
Narrative	Theme	Story	Events	Q & A / Unfolding Plots	Central Truth
Allegory	Theme	Metaphor	Figurative & symbolic language	Point to Point Comparison	Moral Point
Epistle	Theme	Ancient Greek Letter Style	Topical with various themes	Orthodoxy or Orthopraxy	Central Truth
Songs	Theme	Poetry	Set to Music	Response to God's Holiness	Central Truth
Prayers	Theme	Commune & Communicate	Within the Context of Relationship	Various types	Results: Spiritual perspective or Natural perspective

Appendix III

III. The Seven Exegetical Methods

NO. 1 - List Exegesis

Part A: Listing is an investigative study of key words, phrases, verses, figures of speech, and passages that lack explanation or definition but need understanding within the study passage. Look up the meaning in a Bible dictionary. Listing works with all literary forms, but not necessarily suitable for rightly dividing every passage, as a stand along exegesis.

Part B: The List or Listing Exegesis also applies to listings of gifts, sequence of commands, and order of covenants. Ask two questions for illumination:

1. Does the listing reference a [ ] hierarchical or [ ] lineal structure? Hierarchical means the first mentioning is of greater importance than the later. Lineal meaning that all items in the listing are of equal significance.

2. Does the listing reference an [ ] inclusive listing or an [ ] exclusive listing? Inclusive means adding similar or like items for an open list. . Exclusive means a close listing, such as the Godhead: Father Son & Holy Spirit.

Appendix III

NO. 2 - Decode Exegesis

This method works best for wisdom literature, including psalms, allegories, parables, and similitudes which are all similar. Let us take a closer look at the components of the Decode Exegesis.

1. **Thematic Statement** - This found at the beginning of the literary form is sometimes outside the parable, proverb or allegory itself.

2. **Illustrative Material** - Examples, illustrations, explanation, figure of speech used to "context" the theme or subject. Illustrative material provides clarity to the hearer. Remember, some parables obscured by the author limits discovery and clarity of understanding.

3. **Moral Point** (Central Truth)

Note: With parables, Jesus of Nazareth sometimes interprets. This requires the use of the extended decode exegesis - Thematic Statement, Illustrative Material, Interpretation, and Moral Point.

Appendix III

NO. 3 - Narrative Exegesis

There are four components and one narrative question used with the narrative exegesis. You need to be able to identify each of these components should they exist in the narrative and are essential for revelation knowledge.

1. Subject and Theme
2. Sequence of Events
3. Dialogue, Discussion, Questions and Answers
4. Central Truth

Question: What leads us to the central truth? Is it the subject or theme, sequence of events or dialogue?

Notes: Narrative types:
Historical narrative contains proper names including towns, cities. For example, "Raising of Lazarus"

Special Features requires combining exegetical methods.

a. Narratives with Miracles - "Feeding of the Five thousand" These literary forms require both the narrative and miracle exegesis.
b. Prophecy - John 14:1-4, Jesus prophecy about the Rapture. This passage, for example, requires both the narrative and prophecy exegesis.

Appendix III

NO. 4 - Epistles Exegesis

Step One - Discover the major thematic classifications:

[ ] The major thematic classification addresses revelation knowledge about what believers should believe. The doctrine of faith is a good example.
[ ] The major thematic classification addresses revelation knowledge about how believers should live.

Step Two – Discover the major thematic constructions:

[ ] Declarative – For example, "One Lord, One Faith and One Baptism.
[ ] Descriptive – For example, [ ] "We are of God little children and have overcome the world, for greater is he that is in me than he that is in the world. [ ] Conditional Descriptive – For example, "If any man be in Christ, he is a new creature."
[ ] Prescriptive – For example, "Walk in the Spirit and ye shall not fulfill the Lust of the flesh"

Step Three – Discover the applicable "P"

[ ] **Problem** - The problem is more than the statements or sequence of events. It has to do with the classical struggle that exist between good and evil. The battleground is the "Soul."
[ ] **Principle** – The principle is always the responsibility of the individual with the problem with the help of the Holy Spirit (Acts 2:38). For example, what violated biblical principle caused the problem?
[ ] **Promise** – What saith the Scripture, how readiest thou (Luke 10:26)?

Appendix III

[ ] Provision – The gospel of Christ is the power of God breaking down deeply ingrained patterns of old lifestyles and replacing them with new lifestyles unto salvation to everyone that believeth, (Romans 1:16).

Notes: When the Epistle does not contain a problem, look for an exhortation of Christian virtue before abandoning the Epistle Exegesis. This exhortation often is the Central Truth. What is the writer's mental view from which to address an issue or make an argument? Discover if the argument is legal or moral. When legal, the writer cites from Moses, the Prophets and Law books. When moral, the writer exhorts the reader to Christian virtues based on the teachings of Jesus of Nazareth or the moral application of the Law. This helps you decide whether you need to use the List Exegesis or the Epistle Exegesis.

Appendix III

NO. 5 - Miracle Exegesis

A miracle is a supernatural manifestation of God's Power and Presence in the natural realm. The miracle, also know as signs or wonders are special revelation that God show us, with another special revelation in which He tells us. God's (miracle) serves as a compass that directs us to what God tell us (a saying). The Central Truth is the saying, rather than the miracle. The components of miracle exegesis are as follows:

1. Pre-Deliverance State - What was the condition before liberation, release or rescued?
2. Deliverance Formula – What steps brought the deliverance to pass. For example, "Take up thy bed and walk"
3. Post Deliverance State – What is the condition after deliverance?
4. Response, when applicable - What was the response to the miracle or saying?

Notes: Many miracles, signs and wonders of the Bible often do not fit within the components of a miracle exegesis. It becomes necessary to isolate the available miracle components contained in the narrative, so the miracle directs us to the Central Truth. For example, Moses and the Burning Bush, Jesus walks on water, the changing water to wine, and so forth are miracles that need isolation.

Appendix III

NO. 6 - Prophecy Exegesis

Introduction: The prophets divinely appointed individuals must pass the Moses Test,

The "Prophet of Deuteronomy 18:18" speaks of Jesus of Nazareth. Therefore, all other prophets work within the context of a ministry gift. They received God's messages through dreams, visions, and angels, and sometimes-experiencing direct meetings with the Lord, such as Moses at the Burning Bush. The prophets engaged in forth telling and foretelling. Forth telling comprises spiritual insight, exhortations, reproof, and instructions. Foretelling deals with predictions of immediate and distant events to come. Prophecy is a (noun) and means prediction or foretelling For example, the Bible contains many prophecies. Prophesy is a (verb) and means predicts or forecast, for example, Isaiah prophesied about the birth of Jesus of Nazareth.

Step One - Determine the Scriptural Context of Prophecy & Prophesy

1. Proclamation: The passage may contain a prophecy or proclamation (proclaiming) revelation truths, such as preaching, speaking, telling about the God of Creation or exalting the hearer to righteousness. "...*Preaching the Lord Jesus*, Acts 11:20; 27."

2. Predicting: The passage may contain prophesy "*And there stood up one of them name Ag'-a-bus, and signified by the Spirit that there shall be great dearth throughout all the world: which came to pass in the days of Claudius Caesar*, Acts 11:28."

Appendix III

3. Fulfillments: The passage may contain a prophecy that fulfilled in more than one era. For example, Matthew 24:1, 2, records the Temple destruction in 70 AD, when Titus destroyed it, representing its first fulfillment. The eventual destruction of the Temple as prophesied by Jesus of Nazareth called the "Abomination of Desolation, Matthew 24:15," occurs three and a half years into the tribulation period and ushers in the great tribulation, Matthew 24:21.

Step Two - Determine the types of prophecy:
- Fulfilled – When you encounter prophetic literature during Biblical studies, the reference to its fulfillment becomes integral to the study passage.
- Not yet fulfilled – When studying prophetic literature an "End Time Events Calendar" provides discover of its fulfillment. For example, Jesus prophesied a gathering in John 14:1-4 and John 15. This gathering is not a fulfilled prophecy. The Apostle Paul records the next event for the "Body of Christ", namely, the Rapture (I Thessalonians 4:13-18). If the church gathering has not taken place, we should consider checking "The Time Line" for its fulfillment.

Step Three - Determine the Time Line of Bible Prophecy when applicable.
- Please refer to Chart 10 -1 p., 138 and Eschatology Notes, p. 153.

Appendix III

Chart 10-1

SUMMARY OF END TIME EVENTS

- The Rapture
- The Tribulation Period
- Daniel's 70th Week (Final 7 years of Jewish Dispensation and Time of the Antichrist)

Judgment Seat of Christ Marriage Supper of the Lamb	Two witnesses 144,000 Jewish Evangelists	Battle of Armageddon Judgment of the Living Nations

- The Millennial Reign of Jesus - The Second Coming

Satan Bound in the Bottomless Pit	Day of the Lord

- Transition from last Millennium to Eternal State

Satan Released for a Short Time	Satan Cast into the Lake of Fire	Great White Throne Judgment	Earth Purified by Fire

- Eternity Future – New Heaven & New Earth Heavenly Jerusalem Transported to Earth – Day of God

Appendix III

NO. 7 - Prayer Exegesis

The act of praying stands for a relationship in which prayer is an act of worship. Prophetic Prayer has four components:

- COMMUNION – Listen to God speaks, for example, Scriptures, preaching, bible study.
- COMMUNICATION – Talk, petition, give thanks.
- FELLOWSHIP with God - Communion and Communication only operates within the context of this fellowship, in Faith expecting results.
- EXEGETICAL CONSIDERATIONS

   A. Does the Prayer have the right standing (justification) and status (sanctification) with which to pray?
   [ ] Yes   [ ] No

   Scripture _____

   B. Does the Text contain evidence of communion with God?
   [ ] Yes   [ ] No

   Scripture _____

   C. Does the Text indicate an answer to the Prayer or (Prophetic Prayer)?
   [ ] Yes   [ ] No

   Scripture _____

   [ ] Unknown

   D. Identify the elements of the prayer.

Index of Charts

Charts	Page
Chart 1-1 KINGDOM/COVENANT PRINCIPLES	27
Chart 2-2 PARALLEL OR SYNOPTIC ACCOUNTS	28
Chart 3-3 RESULTS OF JESUS REJECTION	29
Chart 4-4 JESUS HIERARCHY AUTHORITY CLAIMS	33
Chart 5-5 CIRCLES OF INFLUENCE	34
Chart 6-6 THE KINGDOM OF HEAVEN	38
Chart 7-7 WHO IS APOSTLE PAUL?	48
Chart 8-8 JESUS "I AM" SAYINGS	58
Chart 9-9 ABRAHAM TALKS WITH GOD	68
Chart 10-1 SUMMARY OF END TIME EVENTS	138
Chart 10-2 NARRATIVE TYPES	74

Index of Exegesis

BASIC INFO	SCRIPTURE	PAGE
Text	Matthew 13:31-32	23
Context	Matthew 13: 31b -32	24
Literary Form	*Parable*	24
Background	Matthew 13:1-53	28
Panoramic View	Book of Matthew	29
Exegesis	*Decode Exegesis*	36
Central Truth	Matthew 13:31b-32	37

[ ]

Text	I Corinthians 9:2	45
Context	I Corinthians 9:1-14	45
Literary Form	*Epistle*	45
Background	I Corinthians 9:1-27	47
Panoramic View	I & II Corinthians	47
Exegesis	*List Exegesis*	49
Central Truth	I Corinthians 9:2	52

[ ]

Text	John 10:10	55
Context	John 10: 1-21	55
Literary Form	*Parable*	55
Background	John 8:1 - 10:21	57
Panoramic View	Book of John, I, II and III Epistle and Book of Revelation	57
Exegesis	*Decode Exegesis*	62
Central Truth	John 10:9	63

Index of Exegesis

BASIC INFO	SCRIPTURE	PAGE
Text	Genesis 18:25	65
Context	Genesis 18:16-33	65
Literary Form	*Historical Narrative*	65
Background	Genesis 18:1 - 20:18	66
Panoramic View	Pentateuch	66
Exegesis	*Narrative Exegesis*	73
Central Truth	Genesis 18:25	74

[ ]

Text	Galatians 3:10-14	77
Context	Galatians 3:10-14	78
Literary Form	*Epistle*	78
Background	Galatians 3:10-4:11	79
Panoramic View	Book of Galatians	80
Exegesis	*Epistle Exegesis*	82
Central Truth	Galatians 3:13	83

[ ]

Text	John 2:11	86
Context	(John 2:1-12	86
Literary Form	*Narrative with Miracle*	86
Background	John 2:1-12	87
Panoramic View	Book of John, I, II, and III Epistle of John and the Book of Revelations	87
Exegesis	*Miracle Exegesis*	91
Central Truth	John 2:11b	91

Index of Exegesis

BASIC INFO	SCRIPTURE	PAGE
Text	Matthew 25:34	94
Context	Matthew 25:31-46	94
Literary Form	*Prophetic Narrative*	95
Background	Matthew 24:1 - 25:46)	95
Panoramic View	Book of Matthew	96
Exegesis	*Prophecy Exegesis*	101
Central Truth	Mathew 25:46	101

[ ]

Text	Ephesians 1:22-23	104
Context	Ephesians 1: 15-23	104
Literary Form	*Epistle with Prayer*	105
Background	Ephesians 1: 15-23	106
Panoramic View	Book of Ephesians	106
Exegesis	*Prayer Exegesis*	109
Central Truth	Ephesians 1:17	110

Index of Figures of Speech

Antiptosis
- Galatians 3:14 p. 81.
- Ephesians 1:18 p. 107.

Anthropopatheia
- John 10:11 p. 60.
- Genesis 18:21 p. 70.
- Genesis 18:22 p. 71.

Ampliatio
– John 10:16 p. 61.

Dialogismos
- Matthew 25:37-39 p. 99.

Ellipsis
- 1 Corinthians 9:4 p. 50.
- 1 Corinthians 9:10 p. 51.

Epitrechon
- John 2:9 p. 90.

Erotesis
- 1 Corinthians 9:7 p. 51.

Erotesis (In Affirmative Negation)
- Genesis 18:17 p. 69.

Index of Figures of Speech

Genitive of Origin and Efficient Cause (Genitive of the Contents)
- John 2:7 p. 90.

Heterosis (Of Tenses)
- John 10:17, 18 p. 61.

Idioma
- John 1:51 p. 88.
- John 2:4 p. 89.
- Matthew 25:31 p. 98.

Meiosis Or A Be-Littleing
- Genesis 18:27 p. 71.

Metonymy (Of The Adjunct
– Galatians 3:13 p. 81.

Metonymy (Of Cause)
- Genesis 18:18 p. 70.
- Galatians 3:13 p. 81.

Metonymy (Of Subject)
- Genesis 18:25 p. 71.

Parcemia
- Matthew 13:31, 32; 17:20, Luke 17:6 p. 36.
- 1 Corinthians 9:7 p. 51.

Parembole
- Ephesians 1:23 p. 108.

Index of Figures of Speech

Parechesis
- John 10:1 p. 59.

Prosopopceia
– Genesis 18:20 p. 70.

Repetition
- John 10:1 p. 59.

Repeated Negation
– John 10:5 p. 59.

Simile
- Matthew 13:31b p. 37.

Synecdoche' Of The Genus
- John 10:8 p. 60.

Synecdoche' Of The Species
– John 10:9 p. 60.

Synecdoche (Of The Whole)
– Matthew 25:36 p. 99.

Syntheton
– Genesis 18:27 p. 77.

Study Resources

APOSTLES' CREED & SCRIPTURAL CONFIRMATION

Instructions: Read each statement below. If you believe it, then "check" it in the brackets. If you do not believe it, place an "X" in the bracket. If you are uncertain, enter a question mark (?) in the proper bracket. Quote the relevant part of your *Authorized King James Version* validation on the line for each belief, underlining the words most relevant. The lines in parentheses are for any added scriptures that you care to record with just book, chapter and verse notation. The first two beliefs are samples: add other confirmation, if you wish.

1. **[YES]** I believe in God, the Father Almighty:
Genesis 35:11: And God said unto him, I am God Almighty ...

2. **[YES]** maker of heaven and earth:
Genesis 1:1: In the beginning, God created the heaven and the earth.

3. [ ] and in His only Son, Our Lord:
(_____)
_____
_____

4. [ ] who was conceived by the Holy Ghost:
(_____)
_____
_____

5. [ ] born of the Virgin Mary:
(_____)
_____
_____

Study Resources

6. [ ] suffered under Pontius Pilate:
(_____)
_____
_____

7. [ ] was crucified, dead and buried:
(_____)
_____
_____

8. [ ] The third day he rose from the dead:
(_____)
_____
_____

9. [ ] He ascended into heaven:
(_____)
_____
_____

10. [ ] and sitteth at the right hand of God, the Father Almighty:
(_____)
_____
_____

11. [ ] from thence He shall come to judge the quick and the dead:
(_____)
_____
_____

Study Resources

12. [ ] I believe in the Holy Ghost:
(_____)
_____

13. [ ] the holy catholic church:
(_____)
_____

14. [ ] the communion of saints:
(_____)
_____

15. [ ] the forgiveness of sins:
(_____)
_____

16. [ ] the resurrection of the body:
(_____)
_____

17. [ ] and the life everlasting:
(_____)
_____

18. [ ] Amen.
(_____)
_____

Class notes by permission of faculty – Professor J. Ken McCartney.

Study Resources
GOSPEL JUBILEE

What Gospel?	By Whom?	When?	Scripture
Gospel of the Kingdom a.k.a. Gospel of the Circumcision	John the Baptist, Jesus of Nazareth & the Apostles	Birth of John the Baptist to the Death of Jesus of Nazareth	Matthew 3:1-3; 4:17; 4:23; Galatians 2:7
Gospel of the Uncircumcision	Church	Pentecost/Rapture	Rom 1:1; Galatians 2:7
Christ' Gospel	Church	Pentecost/Rapture	2 Cor 2:12
Gospel of Peace	Church	Pentecost/Rapture	Romans 10:15; Eph 6:15
Gospel of Salvation	Church	Pentecost/Rapture	Eph 1:13
Gospel of the Grace of God	Church	Pentecost/Rapture	Acts 20:24
Gospel of God	Church	Pentecost/Rapture	Rom 1:1
Glorious Gospel of the Blessed God	Church	Pentecost/Rapture	1 Timothy 1:11
Gospel of the Kingdom	Israel	Tribulation	Matt 24:14
Everlasting Gospel	Angels	Tribulations	Revelations 14:6

Study Resources

Teaching the Principle of Giving and its New Testament Application

CONVENANT PRINCIPLES	KINGDOM PRINCIPLES	CHRISTIAN PRINCIPLES
Genesis 28:22 "Promised by Jacob"	Matthew 5:23-24 "Principle of Reconciliation comes before Principle of Giving"	Acts 20:32-35 "More Blessed to Give"
Leviticus 27:30-33 "Belongs to the Lord "	Matthew 6:1-4 "Principle of Almsgiving" = Secrecy	2 Corinthians 9:1-9 "God Loveth a Cheerful Giver"
Deuteronomy 12:5-19 "Taken to the Temple"	Luke 6:38 " Principle of Reciprocity " = "Give and it shall be given unto you ..."	I Corinthians 13:13 "Faith, Hope & Charity...but the greatest of these is Charity."
Deuteronomy 14:22-29 "Rules Regarding Tithes"		
Deuteronomy 26:13-15 "Honesty Required"		
Nehemiah 13:5,12 "Recognition by Jews"		
Malachi 3:7-12 "Tithe (10%) Covenant"		

Study Resources
Prayers of the Bible

Type of Prayer	Meaning	Old Testament Example	New Testament Example	Jesus' Teaching
Confession	Acknowledging sin and helplessness and seeking God's mercy	Psalm 51	Luke 18:31	Luke 15:11-24 Luke 18:10-24
Praise	Adoring God for who He is	1 Chr 29:10-13	Luke 1:46-55	Matt 6:9
Thanksgiving	Expressing gratitude to God for what he has done	Psalm 105:1-5	I Thess 5:16-18	Luke 17:11-19
Petition	Making personal request of God	Gen 24:12-14	Acts 1:24-26	Matt 7:7-12
Intercession	Making request of God on behalf of another.	Exodus 32:11-13	Phil 1:9-11	John 17:9,20-21
Commitment	Expressing loyalty to God and His work	I King 8:56-61	Acts 4:24-30	Matt 6:10; Mark 14:32-43; Luke 6:46-49
Forgiveness	Seeking mercy for personal sin or the sin of others.	Dan 9:4-19	Acts 7:60	Matt 6:12,14-15; Luke 6:27-36; 23:33-34
Confidence	Affirming God's all-sufficiency and the believer's security in his love	Psalm 23	Luke 2:29-32	Matt 6:5-15; 7:11; John 11:41-42
Benediction	A request for God's blessing.	Num 6:24-26	Jude 24-25	Luke 24:50-51

Eschatology Study Notes

Lesson 1 -- An Introduction to Bible Prophecy

Often asked questions about Prophecy and Revelation:

- When did prophecies cease? With the decline in prophetic ministry [1 Corinthians 13:8-10] was the increasing authority of the sacred writings. In time the sacred writings [John 14:26], rather than the words of living prophets, became seen as the vehicle of God's word with a warning in [Revelations 22:18, 19].
- What is the difference between divination and prophecy? Divination-Gen. 44:5, Luke 23:24; Acts 1:26 Prophecy -- 1 Sam. 3:10-21
- Did Pentecost fulfill the Old Testament prophecy? Act 2:2; 2:6; Joel 2:28
- The fall of Rome and how it fell marks Bible prophecy, Rev. 19:20
- How did Jesus prophesy His rejection and execution? (Mark 9:31-32)
- What will happen on the day of the Lord? (Amos 5:18; Isaiah 2:4; 13:9; 13:11.)
- How will the world end according to the Bible? (1 Corinthians 5:5; 15:24; 15:26; 15:28; Matthew 24:36; 24:44; Peter 3:10; 3:13; Revelation 21:1)

Eschatology Study Notes

Lesson 2 -- Prophecy written for you

A prophet called by God, Deuteronomy 18:15, to be His speaker Deuteronomy 18:18, and the test of his authority is that which he speaks about, 2 Timothy 3; 16, 17, shall happen, Deuteronomy 18:22.

Prophecy as "history written in advance" gives us hope, Hebrew 6:10-11 and the assurance that God is in control. Christianity is the only "Religion" that has Faith, hope and love, 1 Corinthians 13:13, Romans 12:12. Paul's letter to the Thessalonians signals that he is grateful for the believers' faith, love, and endurance in persecution, which refines believers for future glory and seals the doom of God's enemies.

Despite contrary reports, the Day of the Lord has not yet come (ch. 2). A great falling away and the man of lawlessness will appear first. All forms of worship, true and false began the worship of this lawless one. His days will be short despite his deceitful satanic power. The darkness dissolved by light, his destruction, (Revelations 19: 20, 21) happens at the Second Coming of Christ, when his deluded followers also executed.

Eschatology Study Notes

Lesson 3 -- Can Prophets Be Trusted?

A prophet who speaks without a matching literal fulfillment as their affirmation of reliability is worthy of death, Deuteronomy 18:22. Jesus warns us to beware of false prophets, Matthew 7:15. Other examples of prophecies of the Messiah are fulfilled in Jesus Christ.

Lesson 4 - God under Contract (Part 1)

Two-sided and One-sided Covenant
- A bilateral (two-sided) covenant though set up by God and bound by His Holiness, is conditional on man's response [Psalm 1; John 3:16].
- A unilateral (one-sided) covenant means that God is responsible, as in the Abraham covenant, a "blood covenant," between God and Abraham, Genesis 13.
- The Abraham Covenant given in four ways includes *orally* [Genesis 12], as a *"blood covenant,"* [Genesis 15] with a *sign* [Genesis 17] and *God's oath* [Genesis 22].
- The one-sided covenants consisted of the following:
    - Land [Genesis 13:14,15]
    - Seed [Genesis 13:16; 18:8; Galatians 3:6-9]
    - Blessings [Genesis 12:3]

Eschatology Study Notes

Lesson 3 -- Can Prophets Be Trusted?

A prophet who speaks without a matching literal fulfillment as their affirmation of reliability is worthy of death, Deuteronomy 18:22. Jesus warns us to beware of false prophets, Matthew 7:15. Other examples of prophecies of the Messiah are fulfilled in Jesus Christ.

Lesson 4 - God under Contract (Part 1)

Two-sided and One-sided Covenant
- A bilateral (two-sided) covenant though set up by God and bound by His Holiness, is conditional on man's response [Psalm 1; John 3:16].
- A unilateral (one-sided) covenant means that God is responsible, as in the Abraham covenant, a "blood covenant," between God and Abraham, Genesis 13.
- The Abraham Covenant given in four ways includes *orally* [Genesis 12], as a *"blood covenant,"* [Genesis 15] with a *sign* [Genesis 17] and *God's oath* [Genesis 22].
- The one-sided covenants consisted of the following:
    - Land [Genesis 13:14,15]
    - Seed [Genesis 13:16; 18:8; Galatians 3:6-9]
    - Blessings [Genesis 12:3]

Eschatology Study Notes

Lesson 5 - God under Contract (Part 2)

- The David Covenant is an expansion of the Abraham one-sided covenant to include the throne, kings and the Kingdom, 2 Samuel 7:16, as well as reinforcing the promise of the land.
- The Mosaic Covenant given to Moses on Mount Sinai, Genesis 19:19-25 and later confirmed, Exodus 24:1-11. Its two-way terms included:
    o The commandments governed their personal lives in relationship to God, Exodus 20:1-26.
    o The judgments governed their social lives as they related to one another, Exodus 21:1 - 24:11.
    o The ordinances governed their religious lives so people would know how to approach God on the terms that He dictates, Exodus 24:12 - 31:18.
    o Establishing the institution of worship came with instruction to build it, Exodus 25:31, Exodus 36-40.
    o The priesthood, set up by God, is in the book of
    o Leviticus 8:1-36.

- The New Covenant made sure by the blood that Jesus shed on Calvary's cross. That blood that guarantees to Israel its New Covenant also provides for the forgiveness of sins for the believers who comprise the church.

Eschatology Study Notes

- Jesus' payment for sins is more than enough to pay for the sins for all who will believe in him. The New Covenant called "new" in contrast to the covenant with Moses called "old," (Jeremiah 31:32; Hebrew 8:6-13). Because it carries out what the Mosaic Covenant could only point to, that is, the child of God living in a manner that is consistent with the character of God.
- The New Covenant has four terms:

    1. Regeneration - God will put his law in their inward parts and write it in their hearts, Jeremiah 31:33.

    2. A national restoration -- Yahweh will be their God and the nation will be His people, Jeremiah 31:33.

    3. Personal ministry of the Holy Spirit includes those, who are of God and taught individually by Him, Jeremiah 31:34.

    4. Full justification - Your sins are forgiven and removed, Jeremiah 31:34.

Eschatology Study Notes

Lesson 6 - The Parade of Nations

Introduction: Conservative interpreters divide into four divisions: postmillennial; amillennial; dispensational premillennial; and historical premillennial. They are all concerned with the duration or time of prophesied events. This study, however, focuses on the facts recorded in Holy Scripture. Some essential facts to consider in studying end time events are - The Rapture; The Tribulation; The Second Coming of Christ; The Millennium; The Great White Throne Judgment; The New Heaven and New Earth.

- The Parade of Nations is significant to the history of Israel from Man's View Point based on the Monarchy Vision of Daniel 2:26-45.

    1. Egyptian
    2. Assyria
    3. Babylon
    4. Media - Persia
    5. Greece
    6. Rome The final stage of the Roman Empire is the [10 nation's kingdom] led by the "Little Horn," Daniel 7:8; 8:23; 9:26; 11:36; 12:11; 2 Thessalonians 2:4-8; Revelations 13:4-10.

Eschatology Study Notes

- The Parade of Nations is significant to the history of Israel from God's View Point based on God's direct revelation to Daniel recorded 7:4-7. This is a vision of the end of the Gentile world dominion. These end times will have "ten horns" (that is, ten kings Revelations 17:12) corresponding to the "ten toes" in the Monarchy Vision, also corresponding to the current "League of Nations".
- Four World Powers
    1. Like a Lion and had eagle's wings in Daniel 7:4 is Babylon
    2. Like to a bear in Dan 7:5 is Media-Persia
    3. Like a leopard in Daniel 7:6 is Greece under Alexander
    4. The nondescript beast of Daniel 7:7 is the Roman Empire.

Eschatology Study Notes

Lesson 7 - The Rapture Question

Introduction: The Rapture question embraces prophecy about the Church, the translation of the living saints, the judgment seat of Christ, the marriage of the Lamb and the return of the glorified Church to reign with Christ.

- Jesus Christ first prophesied the "Rapture": *Let not your heart be troubled: ye believe in God, believe also in me. In my Father's house are many mansions: if it were not so, I would have told you. I go to prepare a place for you. If I go and prepare a place for you, I will come again, and receive you unto myself, that where I am, there ye may be also,* John 14:1-3.
- The Apostle Paul gave the details of the "Rapture" to the Thessalonians [1 Thessalonians 4:13-17; Romans 11:25] and revealed the need for a "translated body" in 1 Corinthians 15:51-58. The New Testament doctrine is based on the belief that the Church will be taken out of the world in preparation for the "marriage supper of the lamb", Revelations 19:6-9.
- Who will go in the Rapture? The Holy Spirit has given "revelation knowledge" to the "Body of Christ" about this question: Please read the following passage for your personal confirmation, Revelation 3:7-13, Matthew 10:22.

Eschatology Study Notes

Lesson 8 - What Can the Church Expect?

- The "church" meaning an assembly -or- "those gathered out of the world". The best example of the "church" is found in [Acts 2:38-42] when three thousand added in one day. Peter followed the "model of ministry" taught by Jesus according to Luke 24:47 which resulted in the gathering of three thousand souls. This is the first and only model given about the New Testament "gathering" of the "Body of Christ". Jesus taught, "I have chosen you out of the world", John 15:16-27.
- Jesus Christ, the head of the body, *sanctify and cleanse it [His Body - those gathered] with the washing of water by the word, That he might present it to himself a glorious church, not having spot, or wrinkle, or any such thing; but that it should be holy and without blemish,* Ephesians 5:25-27. Without this washing, you and I are not prepared for the "Rapture".
- Next is the judgment seat of Christ, 2 Corinthians 5:10-17. Here you will receive evaluation and recognition for your works, whether "good" or "bad", 1 Corinthians 3:12-15. *"If any man's works shall be burned, he shall suffer loss: but he or she shall be saved; yet so as by fire,"* 1 Corinthians 3:15.
- Next is the "worship" of God for all eternity, Revelation 22:3.

Eschatology Study Notes

Lesson 9 - Israel's Future

Introduction: What does the Bible say about Israel's program of history, its present state and future glory? This is outlined in God's historical plan as recorded in the prophetic words of the "Abrahamic", "Davidic", "Mosaic" and the "New Covenant". The promises of the land, seed, blessings, throne, kings and a kingdom forever are Biblical facts. The duration and progression of these events are tied to terms God made in the "Mosaic Covenant". Israel's cycle of "blessings" and "curses" is based on their obedience or disobedience and the opportunity for repentance in the "Mosaic Covenant" Deuteronomy 28:1-14.

The Biblical Definition of Repentance, 2 Chronicles 7:14
When you are in darkness, [Matthew 6:23] do this!
> 1. Humble yourself and pray ["Father forgive me for I have sinned against thee and against my fellowman."]
> 2. Seek God, Hebrew 11:6
> 3. Turn from your wickedness [Stop Sinning!]
> God will hear you!
> 4. He will forgive your sins
> 5. He will heal the land

Eschatology Study Notes

The Rapture of the "Body of Christ" will cause a remnant of Israel to repent and accept salvation during the period of tribulation, [A time of Divine judgment and great satanic evil]. Apostle John revealed, *And I heard the number of them which were sealed: and there were sealed a hundred and forty and four thousand of all the tribes of the children of Israel,* Rev. 7:1-8. This culminates at the Second Advent according to the prophecy of Zechariah 14. This completes the spiritual and national restoration of Israel and is fulfills the prophecy of Zechariah, with Jesus Christ ruling as KING OF KINGS and LORD OF LORDS, Revelations 19:11-21.

Lesson 10 - The End Time Events

I. The Fall of Babylon, Rev. 18:1-19
II. Heaven Rejoices Babylon's Destruction, Revelations 18:20 - 19:6
III. Prophecies of the Second Advent
   - Marriage Supper of the Lamb, Rev. 19:7-10
   - Second Advent of Christ and the Battle of Armageddon, Rev. 19:11-21
   - The Beast and the False Prophet are cast into the "Lake of Fire", 19:20
IV. Prophecies of the Millennium
   - Satan Is Bound a 1,000 years, Rev. 20:1-3
   - Jesus Christ Reign a 1,000 years, Rev. 20:4-6
   - Satan is Loosed and Leads Rebellion, 20:7-9
   - Satan is cast into the "Lake of Fire", Rev. 20:10

Eschatology Study Notes

- o Great White Throne Judgment, Rev. 20:11-15
- o Death and Hell are cast into the "Lake of Fire", Revelation 20:14
- o "And whosoever was not found written in the "Book of Life" was cast into the Lake of Fire", Rev. 20:15

V. Prophecies of the Eternal State
- o New Heaven and New Earth, Revelation 21:1
- o New Jerusalem Descends, Revelation 21:2-8
- o New Jerusalem is Described, revelations 21:9 – 22:5

VI. Eminence of the Second Advent
- o Christ is to come quickly, Revelation 22:6-16
- o A Divine Invitation, Revelation 22:17
- o A Divine Warning, Revelation 22:18-19
- o A Divine Benediction, Revelation 22:20-21

Basic Sermon Outline

(Companion to the Dialectical Method of Biblical Exegesis)

TEXT: _____

(Scripture Reference - If the passage is more than ten verses only read the text containing the central truth.)

THEME: _____

(The theme should emerge as a proclamation of the Central Truth.) The theme, for example, for (2 Corinthians 5:17) maybe stated as interrogatory or declaratory expression. When interrogatory, "When does the new begin?" ask a question that is answered by the text. When declaratory, "Becoming a New Creature in Christ" makes a statement that is affirmed by the text.

SERMON INTRODUCTION:

The sermon introduction might include brief comments about the panoramic view, background information and the context of the passage. An effective introduction will also offer comments about the contextual inquiry of the Dialectical Method of Biblical Exegesis.

SERMON BODY:

The sermon body may be listed (exposition preaching) verse by verse, decoded (parables, proverbs, allegories) or outlines when the context is a narrative. The literary form usually determines the body style, such as a three or four point sermon. Please refer Appendix III, pp. 130 – 139.

SERMON CONCLUSION:

The sermon conclusion challenges, motivates or causes the hearer to act upon the theme of the message. The conclusion should always require an action, such as study, repent, the new birth, baptism, etc.

ISBN 1412003180